MEDIA GLOBALISATION : TOWARDS HOMOGENEITY OR HETEROGENEITY

EDITORS- DR. IRENE L | INDIRA N | DR. LALREMRUATI K& DR. DHEERAJ K

Contents

Preface

The word "globalization" has been widely promulgated to refer to aspects of development mostly from an economic perspective; to describe the increasing flow across borders of labor, capital, goods and services, and the formation of international production networks as represented in multinational enterprises, for example. Since the 1990s, however, the term has been picked up by scholars from a wide variety of disciplines, such as sociology, political science, anthropology and cultural studies. Its use is no longer limited to economics and the term has spurred debate in various areas of study.

This point of debate can actually be wide-ranging in reach. By way of example, if we look at the table of contents in Global Sociology (Cohen and Kennedy 2000), which is regarded a textbook on globalization, the following chapter headings appear: Modernity; The Changing World of Work; Nation States; Global Inequalities: Gender, Race and Class; TNCs, Uneven Development; Failures of Global Control; Asia Pacific; Population Pressures and Migration; Tourism; Consuming Culture; Media and Communication; Urban Life; Social Movements; Challenges to a Gendered World; The Green Movement; and Identities and Belonging. These chapters might surprise those whose specialties are not in sociology. Here, we find that the word "globalization" is not used in a limited sense to refer to a particular matter (e.g. "the globalization of finance"). Common views among those who take a sociological stance are: "All the dimensions of globalization - economic, technological, political, social and cultural - appear to be coming together at the same time, each reinforcing and magnifying the impact of the others" (Cohen and Kennedy); and "globalization is best thought of as a multidimensional set of social processes that resists being confined to any single thematic framework" (Steger 2005).

The focal point here, then, is that as opposed to a specific phenomenon that can be differentiated from another, globalization is the comprehensive transformational process itself, which is complex in its progression in the modern world. In this sense, globalization in sociology strongly possesses the character of broader questioning from a critical standpoint, regarding the issue, "What kind of period is this modern age?"

How can regional studies focused on developing countries be linked to knowledge from globalization studies? As demonstrated by the use of the term "McDonaldization" as a keyword in explaining globalization, it is sometimes pointed out to culturally homogenize the world and to be a process that creates a flat plane, free of obstructions, for the capitalism of leading developed countries. If we adopt this perspective, the history of developing countries will likely be portrayed as a process of being "hit by the wave of globalization." In fact, it is often submitted that globalization has brought about problems in developing countries such as poverty, and this can be said to be the dominant viewpoint today.

On the other hand, there also some who submit that with globalization, the processes of "homogenization and heterogenization" occur at the same time (e.g. Appadurai 2004). This approach provides a more critical lead in terms of investigating the dynamic nature of developing countries. From the political and economic spheres (market economy, small government, democratization) to consumer culture (software such as music and movies, products and food culture introduced by multinational agribusinesses, mobile phones), this flow of events that can be observed practically anywhere in the world is entering developing countries. In reality, however, how politics, economics and daily living function in developing countries and what people think about these issues are not level across the world in any way. Instead, transformations are often underway that have never been seen elsewhere before, a result of stimulation from newly introduced flow processes. (Democracy is a typical example of this, in that while countries implement the same system of representative democracy, there is great variation in how democracy functions in the different countries.) For regional studies focusing on developing countries, it is a valuable frame of reference to focus on the unique and peculiar things that emerge through close links with the rest of the world, rather than those that emerge from being separate from it. It is likely that using this perspective, regional studies looking into the peculiarities of different countries will be able to break the mold of narrow, one-country research and present wider findings.
Editors
November, 2022

About The Editors

Dr. Irene Lalruatkimi

Dr. Irene Lalruatkimi is an Associate Professor in the Department of Mass Communication at Mizoram University, Aizawl, Mizoram, India. She is also heading the department since 2019 and she got her PhD from Assam University, Silchar, Assam. Prior to join here, she has worked as Assistant Director (Documentation & Publicity) at Mizoram State AIDS Control Society, Coordinator (Media Cell) for Sarva Shiksha Abhiyan (SSA), Mizoram and Assistant News Editor and News Stringer at Doordarshan Kendra, Aizawl Station. She has completed a major research project titled "Changing Media scape in Mizoram – A study of Social Factors Impacting the Professional Role Performance of Media Persons". has presented papers in the national and international conferences. She has also published research papers extensively.

Ms Indira Devi Nongmaithem

Ms Indira Devi Nongmaithem is an Assistant Professor in the Department of Mass Communication, Mizoram Central University, Aizawl, Mizoram. She completed her Post graduate from University of Hyderabad. She was heading the Department of Mass Communication, Mizoram Central University during 2017-2019.

Dr. Lalremruati Khiangte

Dr. Lalremruati Khiangte is an Assistant Professor in the Department of Mass Communication at Mizoram University, Aizawl, Mizoram, India. She has been teaching in the Department for twelve years. She specializes in New media, Media laws and ethics and Video production. She has organized many seminars and invited lectures in the Department and has presented numerous papers in national and international seminars over the years. She has also been invited regularly for special lectures on media by other Departments and different local NGO's. She also contributes regularly to different programmes organized by the University as committee member. She is also one of the interview board members at DDK, Aizawl. She is also the creative director of the Annual Puppet Show that the Department organizes every year to different school kids around the University community.

Dr Dheeraj Kumar

Dr Dheeraj Kumar is an Assistant Professor in the Department of Mass Communication, Mizoram Central University, Aizawl, Mizoram. Previously he has worked as Assistant Professor in IIMT Group of Colleges, Greater Noida (Affiliated to Chaudhry Charan Singh University, Meerut) from July 2017 to Feb 2021. He has also worked as Guest Faculty at Makhan Lal Chaturvedi National University of Journalism and Communication, Bhopal, Madhya Pradesh from July 2015 to May 2017. He got his PhD in Electronic Media & Mass Communication from Pondicherry University (A Central University). Dr Dheeraj Bagged Best Teacher Award for Outstanding Performance and maintaining high standards in the field of academics for the session 2018-19 at IIMT College, Greater Noida (Affiliated to CCS University, Meerut). He has also received "Pt. Ram Pratap Bhatt Patrkarita Shikshan evam Shodh Samman" a State Level Award for special contribution in the field of Media Education and Research.

A Study on the Impact of Indian Diaspora Films on Transnational Communication: Perspective of "Cultural Hybridism"

Swati Kaushik[1] and Dr. Chetan Bhatt[2]

[1] Assistant Professor & Research Scholar, School of Journalism & Liberal Arts, DBUU, Dehradun.

[2] Assistant Professor, School of Journalism & Liberal Arts, Dev Bhoomi Uttarakhand University, Dehradun.

Abstract

Indian Diaspora films reflect the lifestyle of Indians living abroad and enjoying their own culture in the foreign land and also it represents the amalgamation of multicultural ethnicity. It also portrays the challenges of acculturating in the foreign countries when they migrate and the historical and political exigencies which influence everyday life. These films contribute to exchanging cultural beliefs as well as play the revolutionary role in transforming cross-cultural ideologies. Popular Indian Diaspora films are "Pride & Prejudice'', "Bhaji on the Beach'' (a day to set yourself free), ``Bend it like Beckham'', '' Blinded by the light", "Fire", "Mississippi Masala" and many more popular films directed by Gurinder Chadha, Mira Nair, Deepa Mehta & other NRI filmmakers. These films connect the mass diverse audience across the countries and help to build intercultural &

transnational communication which drastically contributes to globalization. Diaspora is not just a film which reflects the reality of changing dynamics of cultures and societies but it beautifully projects the exchange of multi-foreign cultures & with the rise of cultural hybridism ideologies beyond the borders of nations with a human touch of love & respect for multiculturalism in the age of "Modernization and Globalization". This research study is based on qualitative analysis of data outcomes which has gone through each detail of different case studies. According to the careful analysis of case study based on reviewing contents of different Indian Diaspora films and on the basis of literature reviews of several research papers and many books which also includes (Desai, 2018) the Indian Diaspora cinemas are treated as a bridge which connects the global transformation to become the film of different genera itself. These specific kinds of films are so captivating for multiple heterogeneous audiences that it has created a critical perspective over past decades by throwing light on the social transfusion of different cultures on the global platforms. According to (Bhat, 2022) the Diaspora films have created a new wave of sociocultural spaces and as well as the multicultural negotiation in the world of film industries across the globe. Most of the intellectual audience or NRIs do prefers watching the vivid colour of transnational culture and curiously observe the fusions of borderless globalization which is showcased in Diaspora films and the unique speciality of cultural hybridism over the contents of Hollywood & Bollywood films almost portray the exaggerated dark side of society. In this study the rise of Diaspora films have opened the gateway for cultivating the influence of cultural hybridism and embedding the different outlook which will successfully bring out the beauty of transnational communication in the new world era.

Keywords- Diaspora, Globalization, Modernization, Transnational, Cultural Hybridism, Multiculturalism, Ethnicity, Cross-cultural, Ideologies

An Introduction

The word 'Diaspora' means migration or expatriate. The wave of globalization for cultural exchange has created an advanced platform of modernization across the borders of the nations. However, Media in post-colonial years have played vital & greatest roles to promote cultural hybridism which is the product as well as producer of globalizations. The researcher through this research work emphasizes the captivating & highly influential role of media such as Diaspora films in reshaping the social concept of traditional society. Because of many people across the globe are thinking out of box & adopting the new style of lifestyle but this has left rigid cultural norms behind to transform it into a hybridised culture.

Whereas, the global connectivity & influence of Diaspora films are changing the nature of cultural politics in diversity & promoting the transnational culture as the trends by glamorizing the real life stories of NRIs & migrants. According to the book (Desai, 2018) the NRI filmmakers presenting the classy films based on the unpredicted lifestyle of Indians living in foreign countries and enjoying the hybridised cultures and promoting it as a modern trend in the era of globalization. The famous film directors of Indian Diaspora such as Gurinder Chaddha, Meera Nair, Deepa Mehta, Srinivas Krishna & many others have made remarkable films overseas and have won the hearts of people from different countries.

Cinema or films are the mirror of society and this powerful tool is wonderfully used to impact & influence the societies in different ways. The Diaspora films not only promote the hybridised culture but also it creates a platform for intercultural or transnational communication across the globe. These films are of different genres which are in between Bollywood & Hollywood. While the cultural hybridism in the Diaspora films reflects the debatable changing aspects of social issues such as Queer, postcolonial, cultural hybridism, migration, demographic shift, feminist, racist, transnationality. These are the genuine issues germinating on the surface of globalization & Modernization like mushrooms which are rapidly increasing to break the traditional chain of social taboo deeply embedded in rigid mould of culture.

According to the scholars of Frankfurt school, such as Adorno said that the mass culture was a site of capitulation in contrast to spreading negativity which is associated with the modernist high art. However, the dominant and rigid ideology of traditional sociologists resists any changes which are implemented to advance the cultural practice in modernised hybridised form in the era of globalization. Many theories of social sciences criticised the idea of cultural flow in the direction of hybridisation in order to justify their ideology they consider the traditional culture as the roots which holds the original identity of race while the globalization & intercultural hybridization are misbalancing the social frameworks.

Major Impact of Post Colonial Diaspora Migration

The demographic shift and migration issues are the part of cultural politics which is globally impacting the loss of traditional cultural identity of the society. Whereas, the silver screen of Diaspora films works as the tool to bridge the intercultural or transnational communications which is painted by the multicolour of the different stories projecting the vivid range of debatable perceptions. Some films criticise the impact of cultural hybridism while other Diaspora films show the positive impact of transculturalism in the life of Indian origin living in foreign nations. The Diaspora film shows how the intercultural communication and cultural hybridism have created a common ground for different nations to merge the different ideologies together to innovate the flavour of cultural hybridism for all aspects of global development.

Whereas, the popular Indian Diaspora films have projected the issues of gender bias, racism and different social problems embedded in the rigid Patriarchal Indian traditions which raise questions under the influence of adopting westernization. These films also show the transforming lives of Indian origins migrated to foreign countries are struggling from the geopolitical influence on change in policies of immigrations and change of cultural political dynamics are impacting their livelihoods. The scholar Lowe and Lloyd (1997), defines the word 'Globalization' & its impact as the process of global capitalism for universal expansions of a differentiated mode of production which relies on the flexible accumulation and mixed production to incorporate all sectors of generating global economy into its logic of commodification. This term also means the accompanying or coming together of social, political and cultural aspects for deterritorialization of people, capital and culture that is globalization.

Intercultural communication or transnational communication is the product of globalization and it is the producer also which brings out the power of unity in diversity for mutual development across the globe. According to the popular author Jenny Sharpe (1995), countries such as America are considered as the multicultural land in the age of globalization. It is the modern hub of people living in blurred distinction between racial and racial mask of emphasis and hybridised ethnicity. These are the identities formed around the idea of the United States of America as the country of mutable culture & unmeltable immigrants. However, Diaspora as the mixed culture has provided a unique and complex framework for theorizing nation, race and transnationality in reference to cultural identity on the global platform. The writer David Eng (1997), in his article he stated the Diaspora can be a mode of critique for studies seeking knowledge production outside of a national framework as we take one example into the consideration, the issue of queering not only of sexuality but also it is the concept of home through the perspective of Diaspora.

Review of Literature- Social Theories on Diaspora

Appadurai's theories on cultural hybridisation and impact of globalization is focused on the formation and constructions around the critiques of the racial based formation of national identity which has questioned the rooted, static and sedentary logic of modernity. The challenging narratives of purity, rootedness and timelessness, thus the migration or impact of Diaspora is to dismantle the nationalist perceptions & rigid social taboos of belongings that link racist and gendered bodies and space in seamless tales of bloodlines and family to land.

Post-colonial Diaspora is considered as important for expansion of multiculturalism or transnational communication which is the essential need for rapid emergence of globalization across the globe. According to the (Desai, 2018), in early 1990s the Diaspora was considered as the rise of scholarship positing death of the nation due to globalization, Diaspora was hailed responsible for the deterritorialized geopolitical community succeeding the nation-state in an age of increasing globalization. The classic definitions associate the Diaspora with nostalgia for the homeland however, in the contemporary world the Diaspora is more likely to be associated with migration & transnationality but also used the term interchangeably with other terms such as immigrant, exile and refugee.

According to the black British cultural studies, the work of Stuart Hall (1993) and Paul Gilroy (1990-2000), in their theories of Diaspora the Hall promotes Diaspora as the cultural identity which is in the process of mutation rather than returning to origins. But Hall in his theory considered the idea of Diaspora as an antinationalist act and the Migration or demographic shift which is also popularly known as "Brain Drain" is demoralising & restricting the growth of a nation. He also considered cultural hybridism as the loss of identity & loss of patriotism towards one's own nation. Whereas, Gilroy emphasized the dispersion or migration for forceful political reasons creates refugee crises in foreign land which do not provide safety & security thus, dispersion is the tearful process. Thus, Gilroy asserts the importance of cultural hybridism as racial formations and the cultural processes. Way back in the era when black Diaspora was considered as the slavery in history or forceful migration which was painful for the refugees.

But Post-Colonial the Diaspora in the age of Globalization is considered as an opportunity to get settled in the world's best country such as U.S.A,

U.K, Japan and many more nations whereas, on other hand the migration of citizens from a developing or underdeveloped nation to develop country is considered as the problem of brain drain or crisis of talented citizens who migrated to foreign country in search of better opportunities. As per the report (Kraidy, 2002), the cultural hybridism has become the master trope across many spheres of cultural research and it is also used as the tool to criticize the many underlying rigid social concepts which are needed to be transformed in the post colonial era.

While some scholars view the Diaspora leads to the cultural transfusions or the intercultural communication as a site of democratic struggle and resistance against nation. However, cultural hybridism has also become the issue for attacking the concept which is reflected by the cosmopolitan intellectuals. The scholar Werbner (1997) has considered the current fascination with cultural hybridism is powerfully theorized as a common place and pervasive.

According to the (Utsumi, 2018), there are two theories to look into the concept of social hybridism. These theories are Exogenous & Endogenous theories to analyse the variation in social changes. The Endogenous theory states the social changes occur due to the endogenous factors impacting on the society while the exogenous theory means study of exogenous factors which are impacting the social transformations. The Modernization or cultural hybridism of Indians is due to external & internal factors both, after colonial era westernization has the great influence over Indian cultural hybridization which is an external factor leading to Diaspora or migration. But lack of opportunities to serve the own nation in India & also the contemporary visa flexibilities for Indians has created a new way for youths of not only elite class but of a middle class family to migrate to the foreign countries and adopt the cultural hybridism for survival. Before the new age of 21st century, the Only Elites class Indians can afford the setting overseas and the rich class NRIs were getting citizenship in foreign nations while the migration to developed nations was a dream for the middle class Indian in back days. This is the endogenous or internal factor impacting the Diaspora or migration in India. Thus, there are many theories stating the different ideas and perceptions of Diaspora whereas, some theories justifies the practice of migration others criticises.

Rationale / Significance of the Study

The need and importance of this research study is to find new insights & to get new perspectives about the role of Diaspora films to aware, educate and transform the society to achieve the goals of modernization in globalization age. This research paper reveals a lot of social issues being faced by the Indian Migrants living in foreign nations and fighting for their basic rights which are shown in the movie itself. While the values and importance of cultural hybridism are for the people who are looking for the big social changes and they are ready to face any challenges in order to break the myths & taboos which are deeply rooted or embedded in the cultures traditionally. This study also contributes to get analysis on the impact & effect of Indian Diaspora films on the Indian national audiences as well as on the foreign audiences and their different perspectives to understand the core of storyline and also it helps to analyse the role of Diaspora films to understand each other's culture and to boost intercultural communication on the ground of adopting transculturalism or cultural hybridism across the globe.

Objectives of the Study

The objectives of this research study are the aims to find the importance of Diaspora films not only for the NRIs or foreign audience but also for the Indian audience who are willing to know the beauty of global cultures & often develop the perspective to adopt the cultural hybridism in the modern era or in the age of global connect. Through this deep analysis based research work the researcher wants to dive deep in search of new knowledge from the pre-existing information or data about the role of Indian Diaspora films in intercultural communication with reference to the contemporary global scenario. It also signifies the objective to find out the cause & effect relationship between the two variables (Diaspora films & transnational communication).

Research Questions

The research questions related to this study are as following:-

1. What is Diaspora with reference to social structure?

2. What are the theories appreciating the cultural transfusion or criticizing the loss of cultural identity due to Diaspora?

3. Whether the Indian Diaspora films have changed the perceptions about the lifestyles & life challenges of the Indian origin living in the foreign nations as NRIs?

4. Do the Indian Diaspora films interestingly achieve the great responses of audiences worldwide and its influence on people to adopt the intercultural trends or cultural hybridism?

5. How the Indian Diaspora films impact intercultural or transnational communication in the era of globalization?

6. Do the Diaspora films show why is it important for a Migrant to break the taboos or social cultural myths in order to survive in the foreign country & to bring transformation in changing social frame structure?

7. How Diaspora films contribute to globalization & in modernizations?

8. Do the Diaspora films only portray the issues related to cultural hybridism & encourage the world to adopt the all new unique perspective of transculturalism?

9. Do the Diaspora films have future existence worldwide in the long lasting age of globalization?

10. How do countries benefit from the global cultural exchange due to demographic shifts or Diaspora?

Research Methodology

The Research Methodology is a technique used to identify, select the specific process and analyse the date or the information related to the research problem. The researchers have used the case study method to analyse the pre-existing secondary date or also known as second hand data which includes the already published books, research papers and on the basis of careful & in-depth analysis of Indian Diaspora films to dig out the new insights or the new knowledge in the form of qualitative data outcomes. This research is based on observation, it's a new & unique research problem and this research study is an empirical research work.

Case Studies on Indian Diaspora Films impacting Intercultural Communication

The most popular Indian Diaspora films such as "Bhaji on the Beach", "Bride & Prejudice", "Mississippi Masala", "Masala", "Fire", "Bend it like Beckham" and many more have earned a lot of audience attentions and appreciations over past many years. The Diaspora filmmakers & Cinematographers have made a place in the hearts of audiences and & fans across the globe through their remarkable works. After detail reviewing few of Diaspora films & enquiring in depth of the content the research of this research work have got enormous insights on the beauty of Diaspora films depicting the real life of NRIs migrated from India to foreign lands are portrayed in reels with a unique and captivating storylines.

However, these Diaspora films not only interests the NRIs or foreigner audience surprisingly these films are been loved by people living in their homeland and through the mirrors of Diaspora films audience loves watching the amalgamation of multi-cultures & comes to know the new trend of adopting hybridised culture which is the beautiful product of unity in diversity in the era of Modernization under the influence of globalization. The Indians living in India watching the Diaspora films is as relatable as having a continental cuisine mixed with the flavour of Indian spices. This adds the surreal and unique flavour to visualizing the storylines which is in between Hollywood and Bollywood. Also it is emerging as a powerful medium to connect the bridge of intercultural communication to boost globalization in the field of cinema. It has created the Diaspora films as an art which speaks for global connect & establishing emotional connect internationally in between the borderless mass audience of those who belongs to different ethical backgrounds, races, cultures but intellectually understanding each other's culture and interestingly adopting it as modernised hybridised culture in the form of modern trends which is promoting not only the transcultural communications but also uniting the world in the age of globalization.

The beauty of intercultural communication and impact of Indian Diaspora can be seen in the stories floating in the media presenting how foreigners are celebrating Indian festival of lights 'Diwali' worldwide and Indians especially the NRIs are joyfully enjoying Christmas. The Indian Diaspora films such as "Mississippi Masala" have beautifully merged the taste of emotional touch of westernised and eastern cultures. In 1991, this film was directed by renowned filmmaker Meera Nair. Through this film she painted the beautiful journey of an Indian family migrated from Uganda and living in the U.S south and this film focuses on the story of a daughter of the family Mina, who falls in love with an African-American man, Demetrius. The film reflects the cultural hybrid in lifestyle of the Asian-American families and their amalgamated identities.

This shows the racialization of (south) Asian-Americans by the U.S binary discourses of Black & White concept. However, this film "Mississippi Masala" depict the story resembles to the real social issues those are being projected as challenges which is faced by the people who desires to adopt cultural hybridism in foreign country. This movie runs around the struggle of a couple who are truly in love with each other but due to racial differences the society is ready to separate them.

Thus, the Diaspora films are a tool for turning the racial politics across the globe by normalizing the perspective of cultural hybridism & importance of intercultural communication which are needed in the modern age of globalization. This film is much talked about by the south Asian, Asian-American and American studies scholars especially in the context of cultural study.

Fig 1.Google Image: Teaser of Indian Diaspora film "Mississippi Masala", Directed by Mira Nair (1991).

"Mississippi Masala" celebrates the authentic & amalgamated colours of transcultural romance in between Mina and Demetrius, the whole move revolves around the couple who are truly in love with each other and after all the social hindrance they struggles to get united & overcome the concept of racial discrimination & adopt the beauty of multiculturism beyond racism in the city of Mississippi (U.S.A). This film is a taboo breaker and also fights for the rights black (African-Americans) by raising the questions on the social myth based on racism. This film shows the importance and need for cultural hybridism in the era of global progressions.

One terrifying & remarkable scene in the film (The Uganda soldiers used their weapons to tear off the mangalsutra or necklace (the necklace which symbolizes the Indianness of a married women) of Kinnu, the mother of Mina) reflects the anxieties regarding the Asians who are socially and culturally separated from the Africans across the racial, social, class and gender divide established by the colonial rule and in persisting of postcolonial independence.

Whereas the portrayal of African nation-state man as a masculine and sexually dangerous is threatening to the vulnerable Asian and feminine racial minority, which is the issue of violation of fraternity of the nation. This also shows the racial discriminations and the failure of multiculturalism perspective in Postcolonial Uganda. After the horrific racialism incident the Indian family moved to Britain then to America in search of peace beyond the social discrimination on the basis of races. Thus, the film also reflects that America is the nation as the global hub for exceptional possibilities for multiculturalism & for intercultural communication in normalizing adaptation of cultural hybridisation.

Figure 2 Google Image, Teaser of Indian Diaspora Film "Bend it like Beckham" Directed by Gurinder Chadha (2002).

Another popular Indian Diaspora film "Bend it like Beckham" was directed by the eminent filmmaker Gurinder Chadha in 2002, the storyline revolves around a young girl born in British Punjabi family since her childhood she dreamed of becoming a football player, however she falls in love with her British friend. The film is beautiful portrayal of transcultural homosexual modern romance & the true faith in love beyond racism.

The film opens with the story of an Indian origin Britain born young girl Jesminder popularly known as Jess among her friends. Her family is traditionally deep rooted into the culture of Punjab while living in Britain they haven't left their root culture, wherever they go they always carry the Punjabi touch in their personality. While Jess is different from other members of her family, she was born and brought up in Britain and she had the complete influence of her English friends on her.

Even though she refuses to dress like Punjabis or speak in Punjabi language, she thinks and speaks like English people. She always dreamed of becoming a footballer, so after a lot of arguments with her mother she always goes with her English friends to the football court in western sporty attire. Someday she fall in love not with her Irish soccer coach Joe but with her English friend-fellow player Juliette commonly famous as Jules and repeatedly this homosexual romantic relationship turned into the most physically intimate relationship, which was not accepted by her traditionally rooted morals of Punjabi family. The sexual relationship between two young women of different races and queered concept adds the new vibrant colour in new edged form of relationship under the influence of cultural hybridism. In order to gain Jules's family trust Jess travelled to the United States of America to play football matches & get engaged to Jules to become her official fiancé.

This film has linked the concept of an ambitious football player who refuses to accept social taboos & is highly influenced by western culture and she lives in sexual relationship with her lesbian friend Jules and had travelled miles to achieve the relationship goal & to make this queered relationship official beyond worrying about social rejections or criticism, she fought for her own happiness. This film shows both families are concerned with the ways in which sports may disrupt gender and racial norms & the challenges faced by both of them in order to come together. Thus, the rights to have intimate relationships for third gender, racism are the most raised issue in the era of globalization which requires attention of world leaders for establishing global reforms in order to reap the benefits of intercultural communication and the cultural hybridism to beautify the scenario of modernisation.

Analysis and Findings

The researcher through this study has found out the significant impact of Indian Diaspora films on transnational or intercultural communications. According to the careful analysis of case study based on reviewing contents of different Indian Diaspora films and on the basis of literature reviews of several research papers and many books which also includes (Desai, 2018) the Indian Diaspora cinemas are treated as a bridge which connects the global transformation to become the film of different genera itself. These specific kinds of films are so captivating for multiple heterogeneous audiences that it has created a critical perspective over past decades by throwing light on the social transfusion of different cultures on the global platforms.

According to (Bhat, 2022) the Diaspora films have created a new wave of sociocultural spaces and as well as the multicultural negotiation in the world of film industries across the globe. Most of the intellectual audience or NRIs do prefers watching the vivid colour of transnational culture and they curiously observes the fusions of borderless globalization which is showcased in Diaspora films and this unique speciality of cultural hybridism over the contents of Hollywood & Bollywood films which almost portrays the exaggerated dark side of society. According to this study the rise of Diaspora films have opened the gateway for cultivating the influence of cultural hybridism and embedding the different outlook of the world which will successfully bring out the beauty of transnational communication in the modern era.

This study also signifies the important contribution of Diaspora or Migration in order to boost the global cultural exchange. The all new perspective outcomes on the basis of the relationship between two variables (Indian Diaspora films & transnational communication) reflects that the Indian Diaspora films are gaining the trust and likes of not only the Indian audience but also the audience from worldwide and also in past few decades it has become one of the great influence over building the global intercultural relationship on the ground of creating impactful transnational communications in the era of globalization to boost the concept of modernization which aims to reap the fruitful benefits of adopting cultural hybridism. Thus, this outcome states that the Indian Diaspora film is independent variable while the transnational communication is dependent variable which means that due to one of the factors such as Indian Diaspora films is the popular medium to build the goal to achieve effective transnational or intercultural communication. Therefore, the Indian Diaspora is the one of the causes for developing or inculcating the trends to adopt the cultural hybridism and its effect on the transnational communication in the era of globalization.

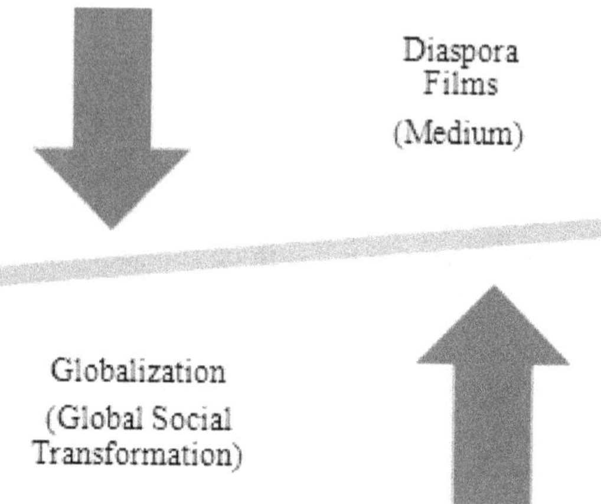

On the basis of deep analysis of pre-existing social sciences theories on Diaspora, this study also suggests that the Media in any forms such as a Diaspora film is the product of the globalization and the producer of globalization or both the factors are balancing each other by encouraging transnational communication and motivating the world to adopt the trends of cultural hybridism. The Diaspora films reflects the storyline of migrants lifestyle based on real cases so it is the product of globalization & it also informs the other part of world about the beauty of diversified culture and the challenges faced by the migrants in foreign nations which leads to the boost of intercultural connect or transnational communication worldwide thus, the Diaspora films are also the producer of globalization or global social transformations. This new insight as outcomes and unique perspective is gained by the researchers while going through this study.

Conclusion & Suggestions

This study is the detailed secondary data based on careful observations and analysis to find out the qualitative outcomes of a unique and new research problem (A Study on the Impact of Indian Diaspora Films on Transnational Communication: Perspective of "Cultural Hybridism)". Further, this study suggests recommendation that there are many opportunities to explore this research problem with different angles of perspectives based on primary data (the qualitative data collected by analysing interviews of renowned Indian Diaspora filmmakers, group discussions conducted in between diverse audience of Diaspora films and also the quantitative data collected and analysed on the basis of responses given by the audience) as well as different methods can be used to do expand this study.

References

- Bandyopadhyay, R. (2008). Nostalgia, Identity and Tourism: Bollywood in the Indian Diaspora. Taylor & Francis, 129.
- Bhat, S. D. (2022). Diaspora and Cultural Negotitation. Maryland: Lexington Books.
- Bhattachariya, N. (2009). Popular Hindi Film song sequences set in the Indian diaspora and the negotiating of Indian Identity. JSTOR, 32.
- Bhattracharya, T. (2018). Impact of Hindi Films (Bollywood) on the Indian Diaspora in Hawaii. Springer, 12.
- Desai, J. (2018). Beyond Bollywood. New York: Routledge.
- Khorana, P. P. (2011). Asserting nationalism in a cosmopolitian world: globalized Indian cultures in Yash Raj Films. Taylor & Francis, 21.
- Kraidy, M. M. (2002). Hybridity in Cultural Globalization. Penn Liberaries, 20.
- Mishra, V. (1996). The diasporic imaginary theorizing the Indian Diaspora. Taylor & France, 408.
- Mishra, V. (2007). The Literature of the Indian diaspora: theorizing the diasporic imaginary.taylorfrancis.com, 51.
- Raj, A. (2007). Bollywood Cinema and Indian diaspora. books.google.com.
- Safran, W. (2008). Indian diaspora in transnational contexts: Introduction. Taylor & Francis.
- Sahoo, A. K. (2006). Identity in the Indian Diaspora: A transnational perspective. Brill.com, 65.
- U Mukherjee, R. B. (2021). Coming of the Age in the Diaspora Bollywood and the representation of the second generation British Indian Diaspora. CINEJ .
- Utsumi, H. (2018). Theoritical study of social Hybridity. Annali di ca', 16.

CHAPTER TWO

Learning Beyond Classrooms – Impact of Online Class on College Going Students

Dr. J. Margaret Suganthi

Dean, School Of Media Studies & Fashion Design

Holy Cross College, Trichy- 620 002.

suganthistephen1975@gmail.com

Abstract

Due to the pandemic, there was a huge transition in the education system with the distinctive rise of online-learning which was the only alternate solution, whereby teaching was undertaken remotely on digital platforms instead of physical classrooms. It became very convenient for the students to attend classes from anywhere in the world as both classes and learning content was easily accessible at home. Students had opportunities to access resources and materials that may be physically located in any part of the world, explore new learning applications and platforms which facilitate them to develop new skills and capabilities while accelerating their growth. While online programs have significant strengths and offer accessibility to quality education, there are weaknesses inherent in the use of this medium that can pose potential threats to the success of any online program. The challenges of online learning are multifaceted. It has presented many challenges to students, educators and parents. Though online learning has played a crucial role during the pandemic, its consequences cannot be ignored. Online classes cannot be accessed by every student due to the unavailability of smart phones, laptops, and network. Unfortunately, the less privileged part of our society has been more on the receiving end of this.

Also there was lack of competence in using the technology, the difficulty in understanding the concept and social isolation. This may increase the class and demography-based disparity with respect to access to quality education. So it is important to find the impact of online classes on students both physically and psychologically. It was found that the students faced both mental and physical health problems during online classes. The study is quantitative in nature and the data were collected from 100 respondents with the help of a questionnaire.

Key words: Pandemic, Online Class, College Students, Psychological Problem, Physical Problem, Social Isolation.

Introduction

The COVID-19 pandemic has caused abrupt and profound changes around the world. One of the major side-effects of the pandemic has been its impact on education with a shift from traditional classroom learning to online learning. The challenges of online learning are multifaceted. Online classes cannot be accessed by every student due to the unavailability of smart phones, laptops, and network. With online learning students faced major problems like loss of motivation, self discipline and distracted by social media or other sites. Online learning methods can be an effective alternative educational medium for mature and self-disciplined pupils but are unsuitable for learning environments that depend on the learner (Emmy Michelle 2021). This results in lowering the student's productivity and concentration. In addition, online learning students are often less likely to receive effective educational supervision and timely assistance (Goopio J & Cheung C 2020). Many parents are concerned about the health hazards of having their children spend so many hours staring at a screen. Education is a continuous process of improving student's intellectual, mental and emotional quotient. Though educational institutions continue imparting quality education for all during these difficult times, many students at home have undergone physical, psychological and emotional distress.

Effects of Online Classes on Mental Health

One of the biggest challenges of online learning is that students were not able to focus for a long duration on screen as there are high chances distracting themselves. Due to the absence of face-to-face communication students tend to lose interest in their classes. As a result concentration levels of students dropped and the pressure to produce the required results give them a great amount of stress and anxiety. Students found that the prevalence of probable acute stress, depressive symptoms, and anxiety symptoms were 34.9, 21.1, and 11%, and the risks of developing depression and anxiety disorders among the student sample increased with the exposure time to electronic devices (Ma Z, Zhao J, Li Y, Chen D, Wang T, Zhang Z, et al 2020). Another significant issue that arises from online classes is lack of social connection. Online education makes the students feel of being alone in their studies, disconnected from their peers and teachers which induced a sense of reduced motivation and effort. A decrease in academic performance, in online has been attributed to a lack of student engagement, with the quality of faculty-student interactions and learning strategies, being among the variables with a high positive correlation (Dumford & Miller, 2018).

Effects of Online Classes on Physical Health

Though the online learning is more flexible to attend classes from anywhere in the world and the learning content easily accessible at home, there are many health hazards to be taken into account. Students spending more time in in front of the screen attending online class has increased the strain on the eyes, resulting in major headaches. The lack of physical activities and constant sitting posture, attentiveness has caused neck pain, back pain and weight concerns as well. Sometimes students also develop bad posture and other physical problems due to staying hunched in front of a screen (Angela Wilson 2021).Sleep problems appear to have been common during COVID-19 pandemic. Excessive smartphone use can lead to increased exposure to blue and short electromagnetic waves, which results in eye symptoms, sleep disturbances, and physical fatigue (Huckins J F., daSilva A W, Wang W, Hedlund E, Rogers C, Nepal S K, et al 2020).

Soial Media and Smart Phone Addiction

Due to pandemic online teaching has become the new normal and university students have relied more on the Internet and smartphones for both social and learning activities (Iyengar K, Upadhyaya GK, Vaishya R, Jain 2020). When college students rely primarily on the Internet for learning, they enter a more isolated social environment. While online learning is more flexible than traditional learning, it increases the frequency of smart phone usage and Internet addiction among students. Recent studies have also revealed that the intensity and time of electronic device usage increased during the COVID-19 pandemic, and was positively correlated with various mental health problems (Bilal, Latif F, Bashir M F, Komal B, Tan D 2020)

Objective of the Study:

The main objective of the study is to find out Impact of Online Class on College going Students.

Method:

In order to meet the objectives of the study effectively, quantitative research method was decided upon. In this study, the survey method was employed to collect data to study the impacts of the use of smart phones by College students. The universe of this research consists of undergraduate college students from Arts and science colleges.

Research Question

1. Are there differences in attending online class and its impact among college going boys

and girls?

2. What are the adverse effects of online class among college going students?

Sample:

A sample of 100 was drawn through random sampling technique, using Israel's table from a private institution in Tiruchirappalli .The sample was the college going students studying in first, second and third year.

Statistical Tool:

Statistical Package for Social Science (SPSS) was used for the statistical analyses of the data.

Tool Used:

Investigator designed a questionnaire and it was used as the instrument for collecting the required data. The questionnaire was constructed comprising variables from the available research literatures. Most of the questions are Likert type and very few questions are of open ended. The questionnaire comprised of 26 questions. The questions were based on of online class and its impact on students psychological and physical Health.

Statistical Techniques Used

- Frequency test
- T test was performed to find the difference in the impact of online class among college boys and girls.

- A one way analysis of variance was performed to find the cause and effect with compound variable, no of hours spent in online class as the independent variable on various dependent variables.

Analyses and Findings

Frequency Distribution based on preference of Online learning or Classroom Learning

		Frequency	Percent	Valid Percent	Cumulative Percent
Valid	Online learning	26	26.0	26.0	26.0
	Classroom learning	74	74.0	74.0	100.0
	Total	100	100.0	100.0	

From the above table we can observe that 74% of the respondents prefer classroom learning which is more than that of online learning that is 26%.Hence the researcher concludes that more number of respondents prefer classroom learning because it promotes interpersonal interaction, it is fun and engaging and clarify the doubts directly with the teacher.

Frequency Distribution based on preference of Family Distraction faced during Online classes

		Frequency	Percent	Valid Percent	Cumulative Percent
Valid	never	20	20.0	20.0	20.0
	somewhat	37	37.0	37.0	57.0
	often	25	25.0	25.0	82.0
	always	18	18.0	18.0	100.0
	Total	100	100.0	100.0	

Frequency Distribution based on preference of Technical Issues faced during Online classes

		Frequency	Percent	Valid Percent	Cumulative Percent
Valid	never	8	8.0	8.0	8.0
	somewhat	39	39.0	39.0	47.0
	often	25	25.0	25.0	72.0
	always	28	28.0	28.0	100.0
	Total	100	100.0	100.0	

In the above tables we see that more than one third (37%) of the respondents are distracted because of their family during online classes to a limited extent and more than one third (39%) of them face technical issues during online classes. This shows that the respondents are more distracted by their family like asking students to do household chores, helping the parents with few tasks etc. and technical issues like network problems, device faulty etc., so therefore whatever the type of issue is, the students are distracted during online classes which affects their academic growth.

Frequency Distribution based on preference of Communication Gap in Online classes

		Frequency	Percent	Valid Percent	Cumulative Percent
Valid	never	11	11.0	11.0	11.0
	somewhat	36	36.0	36.0	47.0
	often	28	28.0	28.0	75.0
	always	25	25.0	25.0	100.0
	Total	100	100.0	100.0	

Frequency Distribution based on preference of Feeling Lonely in your online classes

		Frequency	Percent	Valid Percent	Cumulative Percent
Valid	Never	26	26.0	26.0	26.0
	Somewhat	22	22.0	22.0	48.0
	Often	16	16.0	16.0	64.0
	Always	36	36.0	36.0	100.0
	Total	100	100.0	100.0	

Of about 36% of the respondents experienced Communication gap in their online classes (Table 1). And about 36% of the respondents feel lonely because of the online classes (Table 2). This shows that there is a chance that they might feel lonely because of the communication gap they experience in the online class.

Frequency Distribution based on preference of Copy in Online exams.

		Frequency	Percent	Valid Percent	Cumulative Percent
Valid	yes	57	57.0	57.0	57.0
	no	43	43.0	43.0	100.0
	Total	100	100.0	100.0	

From the above table 57% of the respondents agree that they have attempted to copy during online exams and 43% of the respondents disagree that they have not attempted to copy. This shows that more than half of the respondents have attempted to copy during online exams. This might be because of the students' need to score more marks. Another reason might be the absence of an invigilator.

Frequency Distribution based on experience of Headache after online classes

		Frequency	Percent	Valid Percent	Cumulative Percent
Valid	never	4	4.0	4.0	4.0
	somewhat	23	23.0	23.0	27.0
	often	13	13.0	13.0	40.0
	always	60	60.0	60.0	100.0
	Total	100	100.0	100.0	

Respondents exposed to online class experience headache (60%), vision problems (53%) and back pain (52%) so this shows that even though there are many advantages of online classes, its impact on health is considerably high. One more reason is that with classes being online, projects and submissions are also online, which indirectly increases the screen time of the students which therefore makes an impact on their health.

Frequency Distribution based on experience of Satisfaction in online classes

		Frequency	Percent	Valid Percent	Cumulative Percent
Valid	very much	28	28.0	28.0	28.0
	somewhat	30	30.0	30.0	58.0
	not at all	42	42.0	42.0	100.0
	Total	100	100.0	100.0	

The results of the table show that 42% of the respondents are not satisfied with their online classes this may be because of factors in online learning environments such as technical problems, sense of isolation and lack of social support.

RESEARCH QUESTION #1

In order to find out the answer to the first question Are there differences in attending online class and its impact among college going boys and girls? A T test was done with the following variables.

T-Test

Table - 1 **MEAN**

Name of the Variable	Male	Female
Hours spent for online class	3.38	3.88
Able to concentrate	2.20	2.60
No supervisor so copy	2.56	1.98
Affect Job Hiring	1.84	1.48

Table – 2 **STANDARD DEVIATION**

Name of the Variable	Male	Female
Hours spent for online class	1.244	1.043
Able to concentrate	.990	1.010
No supervisor so copy	1.198	1.097
Affect Job Hiring	.766	.707

T-test was done which obtained a significant result.

- A t-test for an independent sample was done with the gender of the students as grouping variable and no of hours spent for online class as test variable which is a numerical variable. The means of girls(X=3.88) was more than boys (X=3.38) was significant [t(95.109)=2.178; p=0.032].
- A t-test for an independent sample was done with the gender of the students as grouping variable and able to concentrate as test variable which is a numerical variable. The means of girs (X=2.60) was more than boys (X=2.20) was significant [t(97.959)=2.000; p=0.04].
- A t-test for an independent sample was done with the gender of the students as grouping variable and no supervisor so copy as test variable which is a numerical variable. The means of girls(X=2.56) was more than boys (X=1.98) was significant [t(97.252)=2.525; p=0.013].
- A t-test for an independent sample was done with the gender of the students as grouping variable and job opportunities as test variable which is a numerical variable. The means of girls(X=1.84) was more than

boys (X=1.48) was significant [t(97.381)=2.443; p=0.016].

RESULT

- The college going girls spend more hours in attending online classes when compared to boys. Since boys have more freedom to go around with their friends for chatting, browsing, partying without many restrictions spend less hours in online classes compared to girls.
- Boys when compared to girls get easily distracted due to their involvement in fun activities like playing online games chatting along with their friends watching videos during online classes. Girls are more responsible and sincere in attending online classes are able to concentrate more than boys.
- Boys when compared to girls do not have the necessary knowledge for not being regular to online classes don't have the answers to the questions in the exam. Because they do not want to fail and lack of presence of a supervisor in online exam encourages them to copy
- Girls are more attentive in online class so they gain more knowledge and are more competitive compare to boys, fare better in job interview. Boys are less attentive and are not regular to online classes are not competitive enough which may give them the worry of affecting their job opportunities.

RESEARCH QUESTION #2

To answer the following research question "What are the adverse effects of online class among college going students?" The following one-way analysis of variance was done with "Hours spent for Online Class in a day" as independent variable. This numeric variable is recoded into a compound variable consisting of three conditions namely Low Attendee (n=40), Moderate Attendee (n=32) and High Attendee (n=28).

ONE WAY ANOVA

S .No	Dependent variable	F value	Sig. value	Degrees of freedom Between groups (df)	Degrees of freedom Within groups (df)
1	Social media usage during Online class	9.660	.000	2	98
2	Clarifying doubts	3.667	.029	2	98
3	ck pain	95.600	.000	2	98
4	Vision Problem	3.203	.045	2	98

POST HOC TEST

S.No	Dependent variable	Low Attendee	Moderate Attendee	High Attendee
1	Social media usage during Online class	3.40	3.19	2.18
2	Clarifying doubts	2.03	2.44	2.68
3	Back pain	1.18	2.00	2.48
4	Vision Problem	3.25	2.56	2.89

- A one-way analysis of variance was conducted to compare the effect of no of hours spent on online class in a day and social media usage during online class as dependent variable and the test yielded a significant result $[F (2,98) = 9.660, p=.000]$.

- A post hoc tukey test was done to find out which of the three conditions is significantly different from others. The low attendee (3.40) use social media during online classmore compared to moderate attendee (3.19) and high attendee (2.18).

- Another test was done with clarifying doubts as dependent variable and the test yielded a significant result $[F (2, 98) = 3.667, p=.029]$.

- A post hoc tukey test was done to find out which of the three conditions is significantly different from others. The high attendees (2.68) clarify doubts more compared to moderate attendee (2.44) and low attendee (2.03).

- Another test was done with back pain as dependent variable and the test yielded a significant result [F (2, 98) = 95.600, p=.000].
- A post hoc tukey test was done to find out which of the three conditions is significantly different from others. The high attendees (2.48) experience back pain more compared to moderate attendee (2.00) and low attendee (1.18).
- Another test was done with vision problem as dependent variable and the test yielded a significant result [F (2, 98) = 3.203, p=.045].
- A post hoc tukey test was done to find out which of the three conditions is significantly different from others. The low attendee (3.25) encounter vision problem more compared to high attendees (2.89) and moderate attendee (2.56).

RESULT

- Since the classes are conducted through online it is un avoidable for them to get distractions like social media notifications and the low attendees are the ones who are not much interested in academics tend to use social media more when compared to high attendee and moderate attendee.
- The high attendees are the ones who give more importance to education, spend more hours sincerely attending online class and clarify their doubts more when compared to moderate and low attendee who spend less hours in attending online class.
- The high attendees are the ones who maintain the same discipline as in offline attend online class sitting in the same place without adhering to the distractions. So they tend to experience back pain more when compared to moderate and low attendee who easily get distracted and keep moving out of the online class.
- The high attendee are the ones who are self disciplined follow a schedule to attend the online class whereas the low attendees do not have restrictions, easily get distracted and spend more time in social media like playing online games, viewing instagram pages, chatting etc. are prone to vision problem more compared to high and moderate attendees.

CONCLUSION

Even though online education has provided students with an alternative means of managing their academic workload during this pandemic, many of them experience significant difficulties. During the online classes, both teachers and students encounter technical difficulties. The most significant issues among students during online classes were a lack of social interaction, a sense of being alone in their studies, a distracting study space at home and insufficient data bandwidth. They also feel of being in an isolated environment experiencing more study pressure and confusion. Face-to-face interactions provide the foundation for social communication, the lack of which can be viewed as a critical disadvantage of online learning (Lillejord S & Borte K 2018). Online learning can lead to all sorts of physical ailments like headache, back pain, poor vision etc. The value of face-to-face interactions with classmates, usually supervised by a teacher, is provided through traditional classroom education. Students benefit from physical classroom engagement by having a stable setting for social interactions, which helps them develop abilities like empathy and cooperation. It aids in both their general growth and dealing with everyday events.

REFERENCES

Angela Wilson (2021): How Has COVID-19 Affected Online Learning And Private Candidates? 25th October 2022.

https://elearningindustry.com/effects-covid-18-on-online-courses-private-candidates

Bao, W. (2020). COVID-19 and Online Teaching in Higher Education: A Case Study of Peking University. Human Behavior and Emerging Technologies, 2, 113-115.
https://doi.org/10.1002/hbe2.191

Bilal, Latif F, Bashir M F, Komal B, Tan D. (2020) Role of electronic media in mitigating the psychological impacts of novel coronavirus (COVID-19). Psychiatry Research. 14th October 2022.

Dumford, A. D., and Miller, A. L., 2018. Online learning in higher education: exploring advantages and disadvantages for engagement. Journal of Computing in Higher Education, 30(3), pp. 452-465.

Emmy michelle(2021): Side Effects of Online Education
https://elearningindustry.com/side-effects-of-online-education

Goopio J, Cheung C.(2020)The MOOC dropout phenomenon and retention strategies. Journal of Teaching in Travel & Tourism. 15th October 2022.

Huckins J F., daSilva A W, Wang W, Hedlund E, Rogers C, Nepal S K, et al. (2020) . Mental health and behavior of college students during the early phases of the COVID-19 pandemic: longitudinal smartphone and ecological momentary assessment study Journal of Medical Internet Research. 10th September 2022.

Iyengar K, Upadhyaya GK, Vaishya R, Jain V. (2020) COVID-19 and applications of smartphone technology in the current pandemic. Diabetes& Metabolic Syndrome: Clinical Research & Reviews, 15th October 2022

Latif, F., Bashir, M. F., Komal, B., & Tan, D. (2020). Role of electronic media in mitigating the psychological impacts of novel coronavirus (COVID-19). Psychiatry research, 20th September 2022.

Lillejord S., Børte K., Nesje K. & Ruud E. (2018). Learning and teaching with technology in higher education – a systematic review. Oslo: Knowledge Centre for Education. 25th September2022 www.kunnskapssenter.no

Ma Z, Zhao J, Li Y, Chen D, Wang T, Zhang Z, et al.. (2020) Mental health problems and correlates among 746 217 college students during the coronavirus disease 2019 outbreak in China. Epidemiol Psychiatr Scences. 20th September 2022.

CHAPTER THREE

Intrapersonal Communication in the Digital Age for Shaping Global Consciousness

Ms. Sundaram Ojha*, Dr. D. Nivedhitha**

*Ph.D. Scholar Department of Electronic Media and Mass Communication, Pondicherry University

**Associate Professor, Department of Electronic Media and Mass Communication, Pondicherry University

Corresponding author's email id: researchwisdom2021@gmail.com

Abstract:

Intrapersonal communication is the primary stage of communication because a person first thinks of an idea, a thought, or feels an emotion before expressing it to anyone else. An individual's thoughts give direction to one's action. So, as a result, our collective consciousness, or intrapersonal communication in a collective form, shapes our society and the world. Currently, the world is living an unconscious life without realizing the consequences of its actions and behaviour. However, this domain of Intrapersonal communication has been less explored by communication scholars as it is pretty interdisciplinary and unstructured in nature. Moreover, in the recent digital age, the various platforms of borderless communication deal directly with the space of intrapersonal communication. With the help of algorithms, they can decode the human brain. Therefore, this study has tried to analyse various interdisciplinary concepts and has used the Marshall Law (the medium is the message) as a basic theoretical framework to define new avenues of borderless communication that eventually lead to the shaping of global consciousness. This paper is based on secondary sources such as e-resources, journals, research articles, news articles, and published reports. It has used the theory adaptation method for developing the argument to describe intrapersonal communication in the digital age and how it can contribute to shaping the 'global consciousness' for a better resilient future. The findings of this paper will expand the domain of media & communication studies.

Keywords: Intrapersonal Communication, Digital Media, Global Consciousness

Introduction:

Intrapersonal Communication is the primary unit of any Communication. (Stacks & Sellers, 1989, as cited inHoneycutt, 2019) presents the same idea as it says, "Intrapersonal communication occurs inside each communicator." Moreover, (Barker & Edwards, 1980) further describes forms of Intrapersonal Communication as cited in(Honeycutt, 2019) :"It takes different forms such as self-talk, inner speech, imagined interaction, daydreaming, listening, and emotional awareness, to name a few. It is considered as the foundation for all Communication and a key source for understanding ourselves and our environment"(p. 1 para 3).

Intrapersonal communication is the primary stage of communication because a person first thinks of an idea, a thought, or feels an emotion before expressing it to anyone else. An individual's thoughts give direction to one's action. So, as a result, our collective consciousness, or intrapersonal communication in a collective form, shapes our society and the world. Furthermore, Intrapersonal Communication in the digital age is blurring the borders and we the humans are able to communicate beyond a limited time and space. Digital age has not only changed the interpersonal, group & mass communication but it has also completely changed the shape of Intrapersonal communication that used to take place within. Intrapersonal Communication is no longer limited to ourselves.

However, Marshal McLuhan described the technology as the extension of human senses as McLuhan writes that "with the arrival of electric technology, man extended, or set outside himself, a live model of the central nervous system itself"(Agodzo, 2015, p. 5 para 2). Agodzo (2015) further incorporate McLuhan's work as he says, "with electric technologies, man has become an organism that now wears its brain outside its skull"(p.5).

However, McLuhanian views have been criticised by the various researchers as (Postman, 1990) expressed the mediation between technology & human beings by his famous phrase as 'technology giveth, technology taketh away'(p. 2 para 2). Postman called it Faustian Bargain where humans surrender their spiritual beliefs, values and souls in exchange of knowledge and power with Satan. In that context, technology can be seen as an evil master but if we go back to McLuhan's view of 'global village', are we, the humans, not the masters of our society? It all starts with an individual thought and we keep pouring ourselves out adding something to our outer world. Are we, the human beings, not responsible for our collective consciousness? Thus, this paper has tried to discuss the intra-personal communication in the digital age for shaping global consciousness.

Objectives: This paper aimsto have a theoretical understanding of the following two objectives:

- Understanding the changing nature of Intrapersonal Communication in the digital age using McLuhan's medium theory
- Exploring the relationship between Intrapersonal communication in the digital age and global consciousness

Research Questions:

The above objectives can be achieved by following research questions:

- What is Intrapersonal Communication in the digital age?
- How is Intrapersonal communication in the digital age shaping global consciousness?

Research Methodology:

This study has tried to analyze various interdisciplinary concepts and has used the Marshall Law (the medium is the message) as a basic theoretical framework to define new avenues of borderless communication that eventually lead to the shaping of global consciousness. This paper is a conceptual paper based on secondary sources such as e-resources, journals, research articles, news articles, and published reports. It has used the theory adaptation method (Jaakkola, 2020) to develop the argument to describe intrapersonal communication in the digital age and how it can contribute to shaping the global consciousness for a better resilient future. In this paper, Marshall McLuhan's key theory 'medium is the message' has been seen through a new lens of how borderless mediums are changing the nature of Intrapersonal communication to shape global consciousness with the help of algorithms. Four broad themes have been drawn to synthesize the two variables used in the title: Intrapersonal communication in the digital age and global consciousness.

Analysis & Findings:

1. Understanding Intrapersonal Communication in the digital age –

According to McLean, S. (2005), *"Intrapersonal communication* can be defined as communication with one's self, including self-talk, acts of imagination and visualization, and even recall and memory"(eCampusOntario, 2018). An article published in eCampusontario defines intrapersonal communication by citingLeonard Shedletsky, a communications specialist, who analyses intrapersonal communication as a transactional process by focusing on its eight crucial elements: source, receiver, message, channel, feedback, environment, context, and interference. However, every encounter takes place within the person. L. J. Shedletsky (1989). Moreover, in the digital era, have we noticed how we receive our feeds what we receive? Have we ever noticed that whatever we search once, we start getting recommendations in our feed related to that particular search that only existed in our mind until it showed up in our feeds? While surfing the internet, we might feel that nobody is watching over us whatever we do. Scrolling is only limited to us as if it is intra-personal. However, in reality, something is constantly watching us every minute, saving cookies, browsing histories, the pattern of our thought processes, and every minute detail, which is very much personal, in fact, intra-personal in nature. This relationship of human beings with technology is turning from intra-personal to inter and then inter to group and further to mass communication as data companies store the collective likes, dislikes, and trends for their capitalistic use. Researchers in Social Science domain, especially communication scholars should investigate this changing landscape of intrapersonal communication in the digital space.

According to an article published in science.org now algorithms are one step closer to read the human mind(Hutson, 2018). In the pictures shown in this article by (Hutson, 2018), it has been presented how the brain activity can be used to reconstruct the images visualised in the human mind. Today it may seem that telepathy is not something real but with the advent of new technologies should this not be counted as an extension of intrapersonal communication through algorithms! Thus, the researcher presents the argument that Intrapersonal Communication in the digital age is not only communication within, and computer is not merely extension of human brain as McLuhan said, but it is one step more than that.It is **extension of human thoughts mediated by technology.**

2. Borderless Communication mediums as an extension of the human mind

What is borderless communication? When we try to think over this question, we need to know the borders that existed before internet boom. Do you remember the days when we had to go to Public Call Office (PCO) for making an STD (subscriber trunk dialing) or ISD (International subscriber dialing) call? There were times when we will only be able to know about world news affairs after 24 hours when we will get a newspaper. Even though when television became part of our day to day lives, still we were not able to get in touch with the individuals living in the boundaries of other nations as we are able to be in touch today. Social Networking sites as Facebook, Twitter, Instagram, YouTube, and such other mediums made it possible to communicate beyond borders in a speedier way. However, have you noticed how buzz is being created on social media sites? Suppose, a highly influential person or an opinion leader among a group of peers, posts some unpleasant information or an opinion, others also follow it and extend it while commenting over it and participating in that discussion. Similarly, if someone posts something pleasant, many people will share the same feelings around that event. So, ultimately the intrapersonal communication is shaping the collective thoughts of a group and if it is some big event, the emotions and feelings will create a collective consciousness across the globe. For instance, Bollywood actor Shushant Sing's untimely death shocked people across the country and across the world. Everyone who was familiar with his name felt shocked and devastated and they expressed their grief on social media and a state of anxiety prevailed for many days. However, according to a news report published in scroll.in, it mentions a research study by (Pal et. all, 2020) how the conspiracy theories were pushed regarding above said actor's death for political gain. This news article also explained about 80,000 fake handles to be used for pushing the distorted narrative and to derail the investigation(Daniyal, 2020). So, this was one of the examples where the collective consciousness was hijacked by some powerful groups and political ideologies. Same happened in the case of Hitler and Nazi community. On the other hand, (Shekhar, 2021) recently published study describes the role of social media for spreading positive news and hope during covid-19 pandemic. We all experienced how learning from others' victorious experiences many people could follow positive and courageous lifestyle to beat the pandemic. Ultimately, it narrows down to an individual's choice how he/she chooses what he/she chooses. What are his/her personal beliefs. Algorithms record what we search for and then sends us recommendations according to our personal choices.

In the digital age what we are experiencing is the manifestation of our inner thoughts and feelings. According to (Bobbitt, 2011 as cited in Agodzo, 2015)"the phone extends our voices, television extends our eyes and ears, the computer extends our brain, and electronic media, in general, extend our central nervous system." As (McLuhan, 1964-2008, page 3-4) expressed his concerns in the understanding media how extended consciousness will be used by the advertisers for promoting their products is a matter of concern as he said – "Rapidly, we approach the final phase of the extension of man—the technological simulation of consciousness, when the creative process of knowing will be collectively and corporately extended to the whole of human society, much as we have already extended our senses and nerves by the various media. Whether the extension of consciousness, so long sought by advertisers for specific products, will be 'a good thing' is a question that admits of a wide solution............. Any extension, whether of skin, hand, or foot, affects the whole psychic and social complex." McLuhan also contends in Understanding Media that the world is transitioning from the individualizing effects of print technologies to a global village in which electric technologies eliminate many of the barriers separating humanity. McLuhan (1964/2003) expressed that "Our specialist and fragmented civilization of centre-margin structure is suddenly experiencing an instantaneous reassembling of all its mechanized bits into an organic whole" birthing "the new world of the global village"(Agodzo, 2015, p. 3 para 2).So, the researcher proposes this argument that new borderless communication mediums are extension of human mind, therefore we not only need to use them with great responsibility but we need to start shifting towards our inner transformation.

3. Defining Global Consciousness

Before we define global consciousness, we must reflect upon what consciousness is in reality. According to the author David Gurteen, being sensory aware of and attentive to our surroundings as well as to ourselves—our actions, bodies, and mental lives—defines consciousness in the practical way. Similarly, Christof Koch a German-American neurophysiologist working on the neural basis of consciousness explains, "Consciousness is everything you experience"(Gurteen, n.d.).

However, George Philip Lakoff an American cognitive linguist and philosopher shares his views on why is consciousness so baffling? In a YouTube conversation as he uttered, *"currently our science or our ability to study things scientifically cannot answer the very important question related to consciousness that is what it means to be aware?"* Moreover, Philosophy deals with these questions more deeply and pragmatically. For instance, Philosopher and thinker J. Krishnamurti describes consciousness as its content during his talk delivered in Bangalore in 1974(*The Transformation of Consciousness • Krishnamurti Foundation*, n.d.). He says that our consciousness is made up of its content. That content is our education, our attachment to furniture, to the family, to our name, to the tradition, to our particular experience, identification with a country or our house, the gods we have invented. When we are attached to our furniture, our furniture is part of our consciousness. When we are frightened, ambitious, greedy, envious, all that makes up our consciousness. That consciousness is the 'me', the self, the higher self, the lower self.

Now, in order to understand global consciousness, we need to understand higher and lower self that ultimately creates collective consciousness.

According to (*On Higher Consciousness - The School Of Life*, n.d.), Neuroscientists have mentioned the term reptilian mind for the 'lower' part of the brain. Under its influence, we resist when we face terrible consequences, blame others, throttle those misguided questions that lack enough relevance, fail to engage in voluntary association, and cling rigidly to a positive perception of who we are and where we are heading.

However, according to these neuroscientists' neocortex is the part of our brain that provides access to our higher mind that hosts our imagination, impartial judgments & empathy for others. These are sporadic moments when our desires and bodies are in a peaceful state, and we tend to give up our egos and turn towards a less partial and more universal viewpoint. In these moments, we are less judgmental and more compassionate toward others. This is the state of higher consciousness. Although these moments are short-lived, they can be increased with constant meditation, contemplation, and prayers.

(Gurteen, n.d.) defines, "Collective consciousness is the set of shared beliefs, values, morals, ideas, attitudes, and knowledge common to a social group or society. The collective consciousness operates as a unifying force within society and informs our sense of belonging, identity, and behaviour."

Therefore, now we need to check whether our collective consciousness is working from our reptilian mind, the lower state of consciousness or from our neocortex, the higher consciousness. Wherever the majority of life fall, that sphere will create the global consciousness.

According to the WSEE (World Studies Extended Essay), "Global consciousness is the capacity and disposition to understand and act upon significant global issues such as sustainability, climate change, human rights, or global governance" (Trower, n.d.).

"It is the ability and willingness to understand ourselves and others within the broader context of our complex, hyperconnected world."

McLuhan (1964/2003) commented upon the effects of electronic media that results in the simultaneity and instantaneity of all things as technological acceleration "approaches the speed of light" (p. 464) and it turns humans into "nomadic gatherers of knowledge" (Agodzo, 2015, p. 5). But perhaps McLuhan's most perplexing claim about electronic technologies is his suggestion that it might lead to a "Pentecostal condition of universal understanding" characterized by "general cosmic consciousness" and "a condition of speechlessness" (p. 5).

4. Intrapersonal Communication is shaping Global Consciousness

At times McLuhan speaks of a movement toward a global consciousness in positive terms, as when he writes: "might not our current translation of our entire lives into the spiritual form of information seem to make of the entire globe, and of the human family, a single consciousness?"(Bobbitt, 2011). But at other times, as further cited in the study by (Bobbitt, 2011) he expresses reservations about this development: "With the arrival of electric technology, man extended, or set outside himself, a live model of the central nervous system itself. To the degree that this is so, it is a development that suggests a desperate and suicidal autoamputation ...." Thus, one of McLuhan's key concerns in *Understanding Media* is to examine and make us aware of the implications of the evolution toward the extension of collective human consciousness facilitated by electronic media.

In recent times, **The Global Consciousness Project** is a recent scientific effort to map out the global consciousness by an international, multidisciplinary collaboration of scientists and engineers. They collected data continuously from a global network of physical random number generators located in up to 70 host sites around the world at any given time.

The data were transmitted to a central archive which now contains more than 15 years of random data in parallel sequences of synchronized 200-bit trials generated every second (*The Global Consciousness Project*, n.d.).

Their purpose was to examine subtle correlations that may reflect the presence and activity of consciousness in the world. They hypothesize that there will be structure in what should be random data, associated with major global events that engage our minds and hearts.

According to the GCP website, "Subtle but real effects of consciousness are important scientifically, but their real power is more immediate. They encourage us to make essential, healthy changes in the great systems that dominate our world. ***Large scale group consciousness has effects in the physical world. Knowing this, we can intentionally work toward a brighter, more conscious future***"(*The Global Consciousness Project*, n.d.).

However, this shifting of focus can be started only from intrapersonal communication as an individual is the unit of the society and the world. As Sigmund Freud's psychodynamic theory (Momoh, 2015), which explains that all behaviours are caused by processes in the mind. These internal processes shape the personality, which then shapes the behaviour of the individual. Moreover, the behaviour of every single individual is responsible for collective consciousness and finally for global consciousness. Therefore, we can see the relation between intrapersonal communication and global consciousness.

Conclusion & recommendation:

Finally, from the above discussion, we found some key points to understand intrapersonal communication in the digital age and how it contributes to shaping global consciousness, as the research questions were raised in the paper. Those key points suggest:

- Technology is the extension of intrapersonal communication through algorithms.
- Intrapersonal communication in the digital age is an extension of human thoughts mediated by technology.
- In the digital age, virtual reality is the manifestation of our inner thoughts.
- Borderless communication media should be used with a greater sense of responsibility. We need to start shifting toward our inner transformation to see the changes in the outer virtual & physical world.

- If intrapersonal communication occurs in the lower part of the brain, i.e., the reptilian mind, the consequences in the outer world will be negative. However, if it takes place in the upper part of the brain, known as the neocortex, it will be accessible to feelings of empathy and compassion. Those sporadic moments can be increased with constant meditation, contemplation, and prayers.

Therefore, we see the direct relationship between intrapersonal communication in the digital age and how it plays its role in shaping global consciousness. With our intentional effort, we can contribute towards a resilient future of the world.

References

Agodzo, D. (2015). *A Critical Review of Marshall McLuhan's Understanding Media: The Extensions of Man.* https://doi.org/10.13140/RG.2.1.3714.8329

Bobbitt, D. (2011, December 30). *Teaching McLuhan: Understanding Understanding Media | enculturation.* Enculturation. https://www.enculturation.net/teaching-mcluhan

Daniyal, S. (2020, October 7). *Research paper shows how BJP pushed the Sushant Singh murder conspiracy to target Shiv Sena* [Text]. Scroll.In; https://scroll.in. https://scroll.in/article/975091/research-paper-shows-how-bjp-pushed-the-sushant-singh-murder-conspiracy-to-target-shiv-sena

eCampusOntario. (2018). *What is Intrapersonal Communication?* https://ecampusontario.pressbooks.pub/commbusprofcdn/chapter/what-is-intrapersonal-communication/

Gurteen, D. (n.d.). Global consciousness. *Conversational Leadership.* Retrieved October 30, 2022, from https://conversational-leadership.net/global-consciousness/

Honeycutt, J. M. (2019). Intrapersonal Communication and Imagined Interactions. In D. W. Stacks, M. B. Salwen, & K. C. Eichhorn (Eds.), *An Integrated Approach to Communication Theory and Research* (3rd ed., pp. 321–332). Routledge. https://doi.org/10.4324/9780203710753-27

Hutson, M. (2018, January 10). *This 'mind-reading' algorithm can decode the pictures in your head.* Science.Org. https://www.science.org/content/article/mind-reading-algorithm-can-decode-pictures-your-head

Jaakkola, E. (2020). Designing conceptual articles: Four approaches. *AMS Review, 10*(1–2), 18–26. https://doi.org/10.1007/s13162-020-00161-0

On Higher Consciousness—The School Of Life. (n.d.). Retrieved October 30, 2022, from https://www.theschooloflife.com/article/on-higher-consciousness/

Shekhar, S. K. (2021). Social media, positive news give hope amid pandemic in India. *Media Asia, 48*(4), 368–371. https://doi.org/10.1080/01296612.2021.1955551

The Global Consciousness Project. (n.d.). Retrieved October 30, 2022, from https://noosphere.princeton.edu/

The Transformation of Consciousness • Krishnamurti Foundation. (n.d.). Krishnamurti Foundation Trust. Retrieved October 30, 2022, from https://kfoundation.org/the-transformation-of-consciousness/

Trower, S. (n.d.). *LibGuides: World Studies Extended Essay: Global Consciousness.* Retrieved October 30, 2022, from https://libguides.westsoundacademy.org/wsee/global-consciousness

Reconfiguration of Time and Space in a Borderless Narrative: Reading Mohsin Hamid's Exit West as a Digimodern Paradigm

Hridya Joly
HSST English,
The Alwaye Settlement HSS, Ernakulam, Kerala
hridyajoly@gmail.com

Abstract

Today, the internet has clearly changed the way we relate to ourselves, to the people and reality around, as we experience existence as an interconnected network of dependencies. This study focuses on the reverberations of digimodernism with reference to the youth culture in the refugee narrative*Exit West*by reading it as a facsimile of the present times. It critically addresses the technological mediation of human lives in the 21stcentury and the consequent mobility of social life. The novel envisionsthe world as a unified space with porous borders that couldbe easily crossed. Even while the characters are temporally and spatially bound in a conflicting world, they traverse and remap their sense of the present, future and spatial territory through digital networking. The new adjacency of spatial-temporal extremes signaled through the vignettes in the narrative is suggestive ofhow quickened global communication is. The simultaneity of virtual existences and closeness between distant lands become the foundation for this reconfiguration. This paper also engages on how the novel draws on a global archive of images of war and violence heavily populated by the news media, to make the transmission and circulation of these experiences immediate yet away at a digital distance. It is explicated that,as in the novel, with the emerging fluidity of the present times,identity is layered and everywhere is precarious because everyone/everywhere is so profoundly and irreversibly connected.

Keywords: digimodernism, space-time compression, narrative, identity, homo sacer

Introduction

Today, the inexplicable domain of the cyber world, to varying degrees of proximity, offers many and new promises of connectivity. The internet has clearly changed the way we relate to ourselves, to the people and the reality around. The more we use the internet, the more we experience existence as an interconnected network of dependencies, leading to a possible weakening for the need of anything concrete amidst relationships, living styles, in temporal and spatial borders. This study focuses the reverberations of digimodernism with special reference to the youth culture in the refugee narrative, Mohsin Hamid's novel *Exit West* by reading it as a facsimile of the present times. It addresses the technological mediatisation of human lives in the twenty-firstcentury and the consequent (im)mobility of social life. These possibilities are contextualized in and out the reality of refugees.

A Digimodern Narrative

Digimodernism has decisively established itself as the twenty-first century's new cultural paradigm.According to Kirby, there are various ways of defining digimodernism. It is the impact on cultural forms of computerization as well as a set of aesthetic characteristics consequent on that process and gaining a unique cast from their new context. It's a cultural shift, a communicative revolution and a social organization. However, the most immediate way of describing digimodernism is as 'a new form of textuality' (50). "It owes its emergence and preeminence to the computerization of text, which yields a new form of textuality characterized by onwardness, haphazardness, evanescence, anonymous, social and multiple authorship" (1). The traits of digimodernist textuality describe how the textual machine operates, how it is delimited, by whom and ultimately its extension in time and in space.

Digimodernism is not limited to such texts or even to such a textuality; rather, it is more easily expressed as the rupture, driven by technological innovation, which permits such a form (Kirby 51). However, a digimodernist narrative favours the endless. This suggests that endlessness is the fictional form of onwardness. 'Endlessness'doesn't mean that the story literally goes on forever. Instead, it can involve a variety of similar and overlapping narrative forms, all of which open the storytelling up internally and estrange it from its supposed destiny (159). It can be:

- a narrative ostensibly complete in itself but capable also of endless additions, extensions, reorderings, reassemblies, all of which yield a new sense of the 'whole' while the 'whole' is never definitively established due to the narrative's internal rhythms.
- a narrative form so open and haphazardin detail that it resembles the subjectively endless flux of life and unfolds as though it were.
- a narrative form established as to go on in principle forever, capable of being halted only by external interference and not by anything intrinsic to the story.
- a narrative form that mixes completeness on the episodic level with a carryover of a certain quantity of material into succeeding episodes, so that characters 'remember' and act on a restricted amount of their past, and age as in real time, giving to a very long fictional series the sense of a single continuous shape constantly fractured and depleted (159-160).

Considering these possibilities, the narrative of *Exit West* clearly matches and overlaps with more than one of the above. The narrative depends on storytelling much for its effect, and Hamid makes this a means of generating suspense.As bombs drop and drones fly overhead, Saeed and Nadia, two young lovers from an unnamed city are temporally and spatially bound. The first half of the story is about how war warps their everyday life; the second half is a tale of globalization and its discontents.Due to the intensified social relations, the novel envisions the world as a unified space with porous borders people can easily move beyond. The characters attempt to traverse and remap their sense of the present, future and spatial territory through social networking. Their connectedness through social media and smart phones mark them normal in contrast to their situation.The novel has a multiple, complex interweaving of time schemes as the story opens and closes on many levels and at varying speeds.To open out his novel, Hamid intercuts the story of Nadia and Saeed with short, strobe-lit glimpses of other people's stories around the world. It's a technique that accentuates the simultaneity of time and space in our globalized world, reminding us of both the similarities and differences among countries and individuals across an increasingly interconnected planet.

The author critiques digital technology and portrays its users and refugees alike as present without presence. They live as connected yet disconnected from one another, their homes, and the nations to which they migrate. Throughout the text, digital life is inextricably linked with political life. In the early days of their relationship, "Nadia and Saeed were [...] always in possession of their phones [which acted as wands] to sniff out an invisible world as if by magic" (Hamid 31). Their phones created a link between citizens of the unnamed city and an "invisible world [...] a world that was all around them, and also nowhere, transporting them places distant and near, and to places that had never been and never would be" (31) as the doors did. Digital technology allows Saeed to become a "present without presence [for Nadia], and she did much the same for him" (32). Moving beyond digital presence as a means to further interpersonal relationships, Nadia also treats her phone as a way to access the world beyond the unnamed city, allowing the internet and social media to take her "far out into the world on otherwise solitary, stationary nights" (32).Ultimately, Hamid sees art and novels about digital culture affording perspectives that toxic forms of digital technology do not. The perspectives these works afford create hope for a socially just future of meaningful interconnection (Liliana 433).

Reconfiguration of Time and Space

There is need to engage closely on how the novel draws on a global archive of images of war and violence heavily populated by the news media. The technological component makes the transmission and circulation of these experiences more immediate. The characters Saeed and Nadia are reading in their phones about the riots while themselves being refugees. They watch its doom from a digital distance, thereby proving the same.This is being ironically posited as an 'escapism' from the stresses of life, as they settle into reading it as an escape-route, a key leading them out of the prison of their present anguish into a world of emotional relief. The image of the screen appears often in the novel, marking the simultaneity of modern virtual existences that remaps their temporal and spatial bounds. The simultaneity of existences and the closeness/connection between different countries, despite distance become the foundation for this reconfiguration. The characters' life functions as privileged fragments of their contextual whole, they would refract a total cultural-historical moment down to the readers; as integral units, theyconvey an artistic period that they dominated across to the readers in its evoked totality.

ZakiLaïdi has described "our new temporal condition as the sacrilizing of the present, stripped of social utopianism and experienced as eternal" (qtd. in Kirby 226). This echoes the digimodernist textual characteristic of engulfment by the present, linked to its evanescence and onwardness. This conscious rejection of tradition and backward-looking of what is known to be definitively lost, become digimodernism's blank unawareness of previous time. Its absence is no longer rational or intentional; it's evinced by the post-1960s' abandonment by the Right of 'conservatism', which fetishized the continuation of the past into the present, the world's dominant political ideology. The past is not felt to feed into or inform or frame us; it's regarded, if at all, with contempt, self-pity or any notion that it might in any sense be superior to the sacred present is dismissed as mental sickness, as 'nostalgia'. To this perceptual absence is joined the experiential loss of the future: educational policy favors teaching children what is relevant'now' and preparing them for life as it is 'today', unable to conceive of the differentness that the future implacably brings. Digimodernist societies steal the future, and torment its citizens. Three aspects follow: they respectively address the destiny of self, thought, and action in such a possible time (226). Migration in *Exit West* is accompanied by a sense of cutting off, a surgical slicing away at previous forms and connections. On one of Nadia's earliest trips through the doors, she likens it to a painful rebirth "the passage was both like dying and being born, and indeed Nadia experienced a kind of extinguishing" (Hamid 73).

The new adjacency of spatial and temporal extremes is signaled through the fragmented vignettes interwoven into the narrative. The author shows how swiftly ordinary life, with all its banal rituals and routines, morph into the defensive crouch of life in a war zone, with fears of bombs, sniper fire and armed soldiers becoming a daily reality, along with constant surveillance. As their cities become unstable, they come under greater surveillance at the hands of unseen authorities. These authorities also control the electricity network and internet connectivity. Surveillance is a constant, by both hostile natives and through applications, social media, of everyone by everyone. The space-time compression facilitated by the magic doors (through which they move across borders) is also suggestive of these mechanisms by which global movement has been quickened. In the beginning of the novel, there have been rumors of magical doors that take people away to distant lands. The fiercely independent Nadia is keen to find a way out of the besieged city; she and Saeed, soon find an agent, who promises to supply them an exit plan.The door that Saeed and Nadia enter transports them to the Greek island of Mykonos, where hundreds of other migrants are living in tents and shacks in a makeshift refugee camp. Later, the couple tries other doorways that take them to other countries. Within the text of the novel, migration is always possible, but the text radically overhauls what the journey entails (Ghan). Cities across the world are no longer connected by any kind of physicality, but by magical doors through which refugees simply slip through, to be transported across time and space instantaneously. The novel suggests that everywhere is precarious because everywhere is so profoundly and irreversibly connected.

The Question of Refugee Identity

Since *Exit West*, in substance, is a story of migration, Hamid writes at the heart of the present times as he tackles war and refugee crises.Though less interested in the physical hardships faced by refugees in their crossings, the text envisages the psychology of exile and the haunting costs of loss and dislocation. It explores how we never cease to conjure new identities for the urgent matter of survival. The characters leave the unnamed country amidst a civil war and journey to other lands in an effort to invent new lives for themselves. At a glance, readers might think "the doors came as a release" (Hamid 110), removing the physical "difficulty and danger of the process" (Lagji 2) of migration and would cleave away many legal and emotional difficulties a contemporary refugee experiences. But the doors of *Exit West* demand that those who walk through them sacrifice their sense of belonging and civil rights, as cities—simultaneously more and less accessible to migrants—become prison-like structures of 'sovereign power' (Agamben77) that demand migrants to fundamentally "redraw their affective, internal maps of belonging" (Laggi 2). Once Saeed and Nadia find themselves in a refugee camp in Mykonos, where in the process of feeling variously relieved, frightened, outraged and threatened, they plunge more deeply into the questions of identity and nationhood. "In this group [on the island]," Hamid says, "everyone was foreign, and so, in a sense, no one was," (74) preparing us for an ideal of integration that his characters find attractive yet difficult to achieve.

This new form of travel, which is not yet controlled by any governing body, is "discussed by world leaders as a major global crisis" (Hamid 62). The doors are a crisis because they force a redrawing of the boundaries between cities, countries and continents. The doors connect constructively 'separated' nations, opening physical means of travel and communication, much like the access to the digital city, to phones and internet allow people of these separate lands to communicate and join instantaneously. The novel implies that "without borders nations appeared to be becoming somewhat illusory" (109), but does not describe this as a peaceful or positive process, but instead paints a world in havoc, "full of war" (109) where even though "everyone was coming togethereveryone was also moving apart" (109) as the lines between natives and those deemed refugees struggle against one another. In London, we find a city determined to redraw senses of belonging to keep the rift between the citizen and the migrant as wide as possible. Agamben argued that "one essential characteristic of modern biopolitics [...] is its constant need to redefine the threshold in life that distinguishes and separates what is inside from what is outside" (19), and we see this enacted through the split between London and dark London. Thus in *Exit West*, the city promises freedom and delivers dehumanization rooting on identity.

In the dehumanization of refugees, it is possible to have a warped understanding of the binary found within the cities of the novel, the binaries of us/them and one/other, through Agamben's conception of *homo sacer* and its abusers. Agamben, in evolving the image of the *homo sacer* into a contemporary discourse of human rights and discrimination, turns the *homo sacer* into a body that stripped of its rights and humanity within institutions such as the cities with sovereign powers being those granting citizenship.This institutionalized binary of us/them, one/other, and human/inhuman, is considered to be one of the central toxic myths persistentlyspread by divisive political forces (Ghan). All the political rights and legal safeguards are stripped away, so that the *homo sacer* is reduced to the mere naked, or bare life of a human being alive only in a biological sense, not in a political way. As Agamben insists, in this act of exclusion, the bare life may seem natural, unmarked and apolitical. But it is itself produced anew in this act and is thus in itself profoundly political (53). In order for the state to abuse people within its borders and to make people accept the abuses happening around, the state only needs to make a divide between those with political life and those reduced to the image of the *homo sacer,* acknowledging only their biological existence. In the city/state, citizenship becomes an ultimate marker of humanity, a necessary checkmark to gain the rights and dignities denied to the *homo sacer*, as to the refugees. In *Exit West*, as in Agamben's argument, the construct of the city and its power structures is essential in creating the dichotomies of citizen/human and refugee/inhuman. The city is formulated as the foundation of social and political life, as its founding establishes the critical difference between bare life and political life. Agamben's construction of the Roman City can become any city, whether the western urban cities of London or the unnamed city of the book's beginning (Ghan).

At the beginning, *Exit West* makes a claim that "geography is destiny" (Hamid 15), implying that the fate of any city is not politically driven but as preordained. Throughout the narrative, as rights of different people are stripped on either side of the doors that allow one to jump from east to west, this opening statement is contradicted, revealing a certain sameness in the geopolitical provisions of all cities, between the life of citizens and that of the dehumanized.The space in which the characters inhabit is described as "a city swollen by refugees but still mostly at peace, or at least not yet openly at war" (10). In this first section, with Nadia, Saeed and Saeed's family being the people who feel they 'naturally' belong in the body of the city, refugees are only referred to in non-descriptive, collective terms, and always as a "subordinate clause of which they are not even the subject" (Perfect 190). Refugees are seen only as human-shaped figures that "occupied many of the open places of the city, [some] trying to recreate the rhythms of a normal life [...]Others didn't move at all: stunned, maybe, or resting. Possible dying" (Hamid 23). Their state of only bare life is a natural conclusion, one which those with political life cannot or will not profoundly contemplate (Ghan). While bare life and political life are sharply divided, those with political life cannot truly see those who are placed into the identity of the *homo sacer*.

A Digital Divide of Death and Life

When the government of the unnamed city, attempts to restore order through a "massive show of force" (Hamid 42), the autonomous rights of the citizen which had been taken for granted as an absolute given to their status of humanity within the city, slowly begin to crumble away. As the government becomes more authoritarian, the line between the refugee/*homo sacer* and the citizen/human begin to blur, the latter being pushed into a state more in line with the inhumanity of the former. This is done first through"a nighttime curfew" (43)to limit the physical agency of the citizens, and then, more significantly, by blocking non-physical forms of digital autonomy as well. "One day the signal to every mobile phone in the city simply vanished, turned off as if by flipping a switch [...] Internet connectivity was suspended as well" (43). This comes as a blow even more than physical restrictions within the city. In the world of the text, Agamben's definition of political life as that which exists within and as accepted by the community is expanded to digital life, access to the internet and communication technology (Ghan).

The access to phones gives Saeed another instantaneous door, a portal into "Nadia's separate existence" (Hamid 31) through which they communicate without restrictions of time or space. So by removing this access to digital autonomy,many more layers of political life are stripped away. In order to experience full political life, the characters must be granted autonomy both to the community of the physical city, as well as the community of the 'digital city' of the internet through which online communities are formed and maintained.When the government removes internet access and mobile connection, they leave those who had previously been freed "marooned and alone" (43), and one step closer to the state of *homo sacer*/bare life that the refugees of the city already suffer. The government tells people that removing their autonomy is only a "temporary antiterrorism measure" (43), that stripping away their political human rights is a "state of exception" (Agamben 19). When the governing body falls into authoritarianism, the city will inevitably "turn on its own citizens [until] the one-time citizen [is] reduced to the 'bare life' of the *homo sacer*" (97). As the unnamed city falls into the control of militants, there is no longer a divide between those with bare life and those with political life (Ghan). "Executions moved in waves" (Hamid 60) and at random, violence affecting everyone, including Nadia and Saeed, as Saeed's mother is killed and Nadia's neighbourhood is overrun.

In *Exit West*, to escape through those portals to the west is not an escape into the promised land, but only another city, with more systems built to keep the binary of *homo sacer*/refugee and citizen intact. After moving twice, Nadia wonders "whether the faces and buildings had changed, but the basic reality of their predicament had not" (Hamid 110). This recognition that institutional forces cause oppression, and not a reality of differing geographies, serves as a rebuttal to the text's initial claim that geography is destiny, and this rebuttal follows the migrants through the doors to each location where they seek safety and the return of personal agency. Though the portals elevate the physical mobility of the refugee, Nadia and Saeed are still forced into that place of "in-between-ness involved in being mobile but immobilized [such as] refugee camps" (Lagji 5). Hamid emphasizes how unnecessary the waiting of contemporary migrants actually is. Their "days [...] full of waiting and false hopes" (Hamid 79) have no bearing on the physical limits of mobility. Just as in the real world, technology is perfectly capable of moving bodies across the world in a matter of hours, in *Exit West* travelling time is cut down to seconds (Ghan).

With the migrants already inside the walls of the city, the city creates new walls between the legal and the illegal, the sovereign power and the *homo sacer*. "The distinctions and thresholds that make it possible to isolate a sacred life must be newly defined" (Agamben 77), and in London, these distinctions are powerfully created, making the political city the powered city, and the space of the migrants, the depowered city. In a passage that mirrors the sharp surprise of losing access to phones and internet, "the electricity went out, cut off by the authorities, [we] descended into darkness, a sharp fear descended also" (Hamid 98). In London, the threshold that isolates sacred life from political life is, once again, access to the digital city (Ghan). Without electricity, darkness and disconnection are everywhere in the sectioned off 'dark London' (104).

The physical mobility of the migrants is artificially limited as the access to mobility is denied to them, "underground stations were sealed [subway cars] skipping stops" (Hamid 101) to keep people from boarding. Beyond the physical immobility of the migrants is the ever-present threat of violence, "nativists advocating wholesale slaughter [...] so much like the fury of the militants" (110) represented in the unnamed city. As the dark city physically limits, so it digitally limits as well, with only "pockets of power [from which] Saeed and Nadia were able to recharge their phones [...] and if they walked at the edges of their locality they could pick up a strong signal" (108) with which to regain some access to the digital community London was doing its best to deny them. By snatching these brief moments of connectivity, Nadia does her best to regain some agency, to remove the endless waiting for information and connection to the world beyond the imposed limits of the city (Ghan).

Even in those moments when connectivity has been reached, Nadia finds herself set outside, becoming the subject of the community's attention rather than as amember. Back when Nadia used social media in the unnamed city, she "left little trace of her passing, not posting much herself" (Hamid 32). Nadia's simultaneous engagement in online communities and her embrace of online anonymity serving as "the online equivalent of the black robes" (32) that she wears for protective and personal rather than religious reasons. Later, this anonymity is stripped away. Nadia can no longer participate in "reading the news on her phone" (109) as a way to access the wider world and has instead become a way for the wider online community to focus her. "She saw a photograph of herself sitting on the steps of a building reading the news on her phone" (109). She does not understand "how she could both read the news and be the news" (109), and this paradox bends her conception of self. Her fear that moving past that moment would "split [her] into two Nadia's, and one would stay on the steps" for all to see, forever.This split between "two different selves" (109) is a split between the image of self that Nadia could control, and the image of her that the city, both real and digital, has created and controls. When Nadia "zoomed in on the image and saw that the woman in black robes [...] was not actually her" (109), this does not necessarily free or allow her regain the autonomy of her online identity. The Sovereign power, which has revealed itself to be a digital as well as physical force, does not discriminate between the different bodies of the refugees it seeks to dehumanize. So long as she remains in the city, Nadia, in the gaze of power, will remain indistinguishable from another migrant (Ghan).

When Saeed and Nadia choose to migrate a final time, they do so right as London seems on the cusp of accepting migrants, but still others them, building new settlements apart from that to be given to the natives with full political rights within the state. Instead, they choose to migrate through a door to "the new city of Marin" (Hamid 130), hoping to rekindle their relationship, and perhaps finally find some escape from the abusive binary of bare life and political life.In Marin, they reach a place with almost no city structure, and no city legacy. In most technical ways, this 'new city' is barely a city at all, but a settlement of migrants. Here, in a realm of almost no citizens, the binary of nativity and newcomer does not fall away, as it evolves into layers of nativity which different people claim in different ways, but the absolute reign of the citizen is no longer supreme. It is not necessarily a place where one might regain the autonomy of political life, but a place entirely outside the binary, and a place where people might at least regain their place in the community of the digital city (Ghan).

Their shared home in Marin sits overlooking San Francisco, the home of Silicon Valley and the "realm of giddy technology" (Hamid 133). It is a place where "wireless data signals were strong" (132), and their access to the digital landscape is unimpeded. Nadia and Saeed seem to migrate one more time along the California coastline, this time away from one another. However, this final migration does not seem to be the violent "murder[ing] from our lives those we leave behind" (68). No longer trapped within the binary that had contained them, this move away from one another is instead a reaffirming of their some degree of freedom of mobility restored to them. By leaving the oppressive archetype of the city behind, but remaining within the community of the digital city, Nadia and Saeed have moved beyond the realm of the *homo sacer*, regaining power over themselves, if not power over the world (Ghan).

Conclusion

By mixing the real and the surreal, Hamid creates a fictional universe that captures the global perils beneath today's headlines, while at the same time paints a dystopian portrait of what might lie down the road. However, though "freedom of movement has erroneously implied freedom" (Lagji 4) within the novel, the power of the doors moves the spaces of the city away from gathering places of culture, hope, and emphasizes the city as the place of violence, judgment, and the institutionalized power of the state (Ghan). In *Exit West*, cities exist in powerful vacuums from one another, worlds of their own that do not connect with each other, that "exacerbate the existing unequal power dynamics between the global north and global south" (Lagji 2).

This thesis explicates the novel as representing the unrest of our times. The world in *Exit West* is, in many respects, is an extrapolation of the world we live in, with wars between varied regions turning cities into war zones; with political crises, hasty technological changes, and growing tensions between nativists and migrants threatening to upend million lives.The non-specific locale intensifies the allegorical atmosphere of the novel.No characters other than Saeed and Nadia are named; even the country remain unnamed. It is given vague cultural markers but is never identified within the text. A text, though, must have boundaries and a history, in the same way that the distinction between "life" and "a life" ascribes to the latter physical circumscription and biography. This novel exemplifies how anonymity is an extension of the universal and also the digital.

Hamid writes, in many places "the apocalypse appeared to have arrived and yet it was not apocalyptic, which is to say that while the changes were jarring they were not the end, people found things to do and ways to be and people to be with, and plausible desirable futures began to emerge, unimaginable previously, but not unimaginable now" (147). The exit in the novel presents an (online or otherwise) alternative to these mass institutions that dominate modern life and opens up possibilities to analyse the present. The novel has its conclusion asserting "We are all migrants through time", and Saeed feeling that "it might be possible, in the face of death, to believe in humanity's potential for building a better world". The end of *Exit West* feels like anoutline for humanity, a path out of theterrible political squabbling and towards a more socially balanced future. This is edifying to the writer's remark that "putting forth an optimistic vision like that, makes that vision, in some small way, more likely to come true" (Hamid Interview).

Works Cited

Agamben, Georgio. *Homo Sacer: Sovereign Power and Bare Life.* Translated by Daniel Heller-Roazen. Stanford UP, 1998.

Ghan, Ben Berman. "Freedom in the Physical and Digital City: Mohsin Hamid's *Exit West.*" *Empty Mirror*, 14 Feb 2020, www.emptymirrorbooks.com/literature/exit-west-mohsin-hamid. Accessed 23 Sep. 2022.

Hamid, Mohsin. *Exit West: a Novel.* New York: Riverhead Books, 2017.

Hamid, Mohsin. "It's Important Not to Live One's Life Gazing Towards the Future". Interview by Alex Preston. *The Guardian*, 11 Aug. 2018, www.theguardian.com/books/2018/aug/11/mohsin-hamid-exit-west-interview. Accessed 23 Sep. 2022.

Kirby, Alan. *Digimodernism: How New Technologies Dismantle the Postmodern and Reconfigure Our Culture.* New York: The Continuum, 2009.

Lagji, Amanda. "Waiting in Motion: Mapping Postcolonial Fiction, New Mobilities, and Migration through Mohsin Hamid's *Exit West.*" *Mobilities*, vol. 14, no. 2, 2018, pp. 1–15.

Naydan, Liliana M. 'Digital Screens and National Divides in Mohsin Hamid's *Exit West.*' *Studies in the Novel*, vol. 51, no. 3, 2019, pp. 433-451. *Gale Academic OneFile*, link.gale.com/apps/doc/A600918138/AONE?u=anon~f8af7756&sid=googleScholar&xid=76dfa1c7. Accessed 25 Sept. 2022.

Perfect, Michael. "'Black Holes in the Fabric of the Nation': Refugees in Mohsin Hamid's *Exit West*." *Journal for Cultural Research*, vol. 23, no. 2, Mar. 2019, pp. 187–201.

CHAPTER FIVE

A Study of Newspaper Illustrations in Assembly Elections of Punjab and Uttar Pradesh

Dr. Amita

Asst. Professor, Department of Journalism and Mass Communication, BHU,

Varanasi, UP, India

amitamgarh07@gmail.com

Kirti Khanna

Ph.D. Research Scholar, Department of Journalism and Mass Communication, BHU,

Varanasi, UP, India

kirrtikhanna@gmail.com

Abstract:

Pictorial representation of the contemporary situations have always drawn the attention of human kind. From tracing the lives of ancient humans through cave paintings to designing 3D animations. Among all the forms of pictorial representation like drawing and paintings, illustrations (cartoons) enjoy the privilege of being direct, to the point, harsh with a pinch of humor. Illustrations are an integral part of any newspaper, often placed in the corner in a box, filled with bright colors, leaves a huge impact on the readers. Illustrations marks way back as far as Paleolithic age, as evidenced by ancient cave paintings to their modern use to symbolize, satire or to create humor on existing social, political and economic situations. The beginning of this century has witnessed a drastic increase in the newspaper illustrations research. This ultimately led to the birth of specific kind of reporting with pictorial representation depicting political and social issues and events, as well as the parties involved, in an immediate and condensed form.

This paper mainly focuses on how newspaper illustrations are seen as a mode of setting the social, economic and political agenda. For the study purpose, researchers have selected two out of five states, namely Uttar Pradesh and Punjab, where recent assembly elections were held. The researchers have selected the top two states on the basis of their population. The newspapers chosen for the purpose of the study, are selected on the basis of their circulation,each from English, Hindi and Regional daily. Content analysis method will be used to classify the themes confined in the cartoon representation before the voting commences.Both the qualitative and the quantitative methods will be employed for accurate assessment of the illustrations. The objective of the study is to find out the genre of illustrations and their tone. The illustrations will be analyzed on the basis of Exaggeration, Symbolism, Analogy,Irony and Labelling.

Key Words: Newspaper,Illustrations,Pictorial representation,Agenda Setting, Satire

Introduction

The basic need for communication can perhaps be traced to the process of man's evolution. 50,000 years earlierwhen the Mnemonic stage was in existence,person could remember somethings. Here, the communication was social but the language was not developed. It was about 7000 BC, the ability to communicate gained another medium-Pictographic. Communication took place by drawing pictures(Gupta &Aggrawal, 2001, p. 5).David Berlo states that, "Communication does not consist of the transmission of meaning. Meanings are not transmitted or transferable. Only messages are transmitted and meanings are not in the message, they are in the message users" (ibid). Verbal messages can (not) be a barrier in the communication but illustrations are universal. If not, thenthe artist like John Leech of England, Herbert Lawrence of USA, R. K Lakshman of Indiawould not be able to speak the harsh reality and comic cruelty through their canvas. Illustration artists have the power to make a character, fill them with life which are then ready to travel the world with imbedded message.

According to Nobel Laurate Mac Bride, communication maintains and animates life, it is the motor and expression of social activity civilization. Communication evolved with humans. It has become as basic as other needs essential for human survival. Communication is defined as the exchange of ideas, thoughts, feelings. In simple terms it isthe process of sending and receiving the messages. This process can broadly be divided into two major strands verbal and non-verbal, these strands have further classifications.Humans are visual creatures. Since the beginning,humans have communicated visually-drawing cave paintings, telling stories, using signs and symbols to share knowledge, and painting-pictures to express beliefs. Theseillustrations acted as torch bearer to guide us in tracing our ancestor's routine, food habits, mode of survivals, or even they have drawn the things they were afraid of, in all we get to know how they have lived their life back then.

Human brain thinks in picture. Our brain can process and retain multiple images simultaneously. A phenomenon called Picture Superiority Effect(Paivio&Csapo, 1972), which states that information presented in pictures can be absorbed and are understood in better way, this gives us the clear idea of how brain process images better than words. The purpose of this article is to identify the role played by newspaper illustrations in assembly elections of Punjab and Uttar Pradesh through highlighting topics and themes. The importance of illustrations to raise issues and events to depict political, social figures expressedin the form of illustrations in different newspapers of the mentioned states.

A deadly portion of an illustration is emerged as a potential combination of satire and wit blended with comic strokes, that is able to hit the government harder than a thousand words editorial can. This is the speaking of the cartoonist in journalism. The term illustration is Latin derivation from 'Illustrate', meaning intellectual and spiritual enlightenment. Oxford Advance Learner's dictionary defines Illustration as a drawing, or a picture in book, magazine, for decoration or to explain something. In simple words, illustration is a visualization which could be in the form of cartoon, collage, drawing, painting, and so on. The illustrations are considered as visual rhetoric. Technological advancement and digitalization led to the bifurcationof the illustrations, dividing them into two parts as Traditional (drawn using conventional method) and Digital / Modern (drawn using software and advance technology). Illustrations provide a lot of concurrent information to the readers. The illustration artist picks up the important story and draws lines, builds caricature around that. They quietly sit in a corner of the page but leave a huge impact, they never go unnoticed by the readers.On 9th May, 1754 in Benjamin Franklin's newspaper 'The Pennsylvania Gazette' published an illustration with caption "Join or Die", illustrating a snake divided into eight pieces; each piece symbolized the American colonies(Sarina, 2020, p. 4). This is considered to be the first political illustrationwhich effectively commented on the consequences of disunited colonies and urge to join for survival.Herbert Lawrence Block, famously known as Herblock was renowned for his contribution in the field on editorial illustrations. He has won three Pulitzer Prize for the same. In relation to illustrations ha said that "Political cartoons, unlike sundials, do not show the brightest hours. They often show the darkest ones, in the hope of helping us to move on to brighter times". Usually, illustrations are drawn and fit in the red line border to attract readers attention. The main aim of researchers to opt for analysis of illustrations in elections, as they not only aid in the information but also, they help readers to understand important issues in the simplest way possible. Where researchers have observed that illustration artist don't always use caricature or direct images to point to eminent personalities instead, they use colors and prominent symbols to represent the similar concept, party or issue.

Review of literature

Age of Interrogation and Anxiety, the name given to this modern age. Twentieth century has earned this name due to the scientific revolutions and altering social, economic, political and morale conditions of the society. Academicians left no stone unturned in the area of innovation, discovery, experiments which are ultimately the product of research. Though newspapers emerged about three centuries back but the thorough and scientific study of each and every part of the newspaper started in this era. There have been continuous studies in literature, communication, semiotics which focused on the nature and functions of the political illustrations. Majority of these studies focused on the effectiveness of the illustrations in delivering political and social messages. These studies have been synthesized and clubbed into related variables based on their overall findings.

1. Communicative functions of the illustrations. This variable state that illustrations are used as a vehicle for message dissemination.

2. Formation of socio- political identity and ideologies.This variable helps to constitute identity of a particular group of people.
3. The effect of illustrations on public opinion. This variable indicates the persuasive power of the illustrations.

Recently researchers have begun to employ various approaches in analyzing. (Sani et al., 2012)in their research on *Political Cartoons in First Decade of the Millennium,* found the need of multiple analytical frameworks in analyzing newspaper illustrations. Political illustrations are heavily dependent on the interplay between images and word specific language.

Jyoti, (2013) while critically analyzing the function of visual mode of the text in construction on the theme, whether the editorial cartoons were able to present the theme of 26/11 effectively or not? She noted that the illustration visualizes the insult and offensive act by the Lashkar-e-Taiba. But not the after effects. The illustrations leave a number of questions unanswered in the reader's mind. This work of Jyoti has helped to understand the need for continuity even in illustrations is expected. The satirical and the humorous hold of the illustrations is their USP (Unique Selling Price). Illustrations must suit the contemporary issues that affects a society. They are not merely a few lines drawn with(out) text bubbles and a caption given by the artist is ready to sit in the corner of the newspaper.Talib(Hussain & Li, 2016), used content analysis along with semiotic analysis to examinethe role newspaper cartoons played in setting the national agenda in Pakistan, the illustration genre establishes a tough medium of communication by focusing on main issues which cannot be published easily in textual forms. Current editorial illustrations endure to assist as an acceptable format for exposure of debatable opinions, often with the resolution of influencing public opinion(Kuipers, 2011).Scholars were not only interested in examining the replication of public opinion by newspapers through illustrations but also, they were focusing on the initiator of thought function of the illustrations. In terms of how illustrations reflect social picture, Han focusing on political satire inspecting the Japanese Cartoon Journalism and its pictorial statements on Korea (Han, 2006). Cambridge dictionary defines satire as a way of criticizing people or ideas in a humorous way, especially in order to make a political point, or a piece of writing that uses this style. But illustrations in newspapers make the best use of satire, using little or no words sometimes.To decide the placement of illustration is as important as illustration. For this Holmberg, 2004 employed experimental approach in studying Eye movement patterns and newspaper design factors stated gaze or scan patterns. He found that usually there are two scan paths namely; Conventional and Perceptual. The conventional model starts from the top left corner of the newspaper and proceeds more or less to linearly in reading direction reaching out to bottom right. Unlike perceptual order which is constructed with reference to design factor entry points such as pictures, labels and colors.

Rationale (significance) of the study

In the 1921 issue of Printer's Ink, Frederick R. Barnard's article entitle "One look is worth a thousand words" shaped the popular phrase 'A picture is worth a thousand words.' One can express their innermost feelings through illustrations. But in the meantime, illustrations are not taken as seriously as they should be because they leave a question in reader's mind,andgives the issue a new perspective. They try to present the narrative from other side of the stage. Elections are important part of Indian democracy where the illustrations help voters to take the right call. As the candidates are so busy in letting down opponents, illustrations help us to draw a clear picture.

The significance of this study is to evaluate the importance of illustrations in newspaper journalism. The ideas raised by the artist and their way of representation leaves a huge impact on the readers. How minute things and their placement shape the desired message of illustrations.

Research Objectives

1. To identify the role played by illustrations in assembly elections 2022 and their placement in the newspaper.
2. To identify the types of caricature and symbols used in the illustrations to point towards an issue.
3. To identify the type of content (language) used in the illustrations.

Research Methodology

The researchers have done a content analysis of illustrations published in Times of India (TOI) and Dainik Jagran editions published from capital cities of Punjab and Uttar Pradesh i.e., Chandigarh and Lucknow respectively. The study is done just before the commencement of polling month,i.e February, from 1st January to 31st January. Both the qualitative and quantitative analysis have been utilized in the study.

A. Quantitative Analysis

Below mentioned are the parameters employed for the quantitative analysis

a. Caricature: Caricature of which popular figures that are used in the illustrations.
b. Genre: The researchers have tried to analyze the illustrations by segregation in following genres; International Politics, Political, Pandemic, Social, Economic, Corruption and Misc.
c. Nomenclature of the illustration section.
d. Number of illustrations published in both the papers from 1st January to 31st January.
e. Symbols: The common symbols used by the illustration artist.
f. Topics covered: Topics covered under mentioned genres have been assessed by the researchers.

A. QualitativeAnalysis

The Library of Congress have suggested guidelines for analysis of illustration. As per the website illustration artist use following persuasive techniques: -

a. Analogy:The way illustration artist 'relates' a comparison between two unrelatable things
b. Exaggeration: How the illustration artist overdoes the physical characteristics ofthings to draw attention and make point.
c. Irony:A situation in which the opposite or different outcome comes, instead of the intended result
d. Labelling: Illustration artist often label caricature to make clear what they stand for
e. Symbolism: Colors, objects, etc. are used to stand for larger concepts. The metaphors used in the illustrations.

For analyzing an illustration, it is important to know who is in the illustration, can readers identify them,where the illustration is placed, andwhat objects (signs, tools, vehicles, furniture, etc.) are used. Another important aspect is the timeline used in the illustration (whether a month,ayear or a decade). How the objects used in the illustration helps to identify to the timeline. Labelling is not only the caption but also all the text used in the illustrations. Labelling can be a caption, which defined an illustration; text bubble, a text withing the illustration; thoughts bubbles, it is words inside the cloud as the caricature or the object is speaking something. Symbol is something that is used as a conventional or general representation of an object, function or process, and the metaphors associated with these symbols. What information can be derived from the illustrations along with the view point of the artist.

Date Interpretation

i. Quantitative

1.Number of illustrations.

Name of the Newspaper	No. of illustrations	Nomenclature	
		Just Like That	Line of No Control
TOI (Lucknow)	14	5	9
TOI (Chandigarh)	21	14	7
		Keh Ke Rahenge	Tarkash
Dainik Jagran (Lucknow)	48	29	19
DainikJaran (Chandigarh)	48	29	19

2. Genre(Punjab)

Newspaper	Corruption	Economic	Intl. Politics	Pandemic	Political	Social	Misc.
TOI	||	₩₩	₩₩	₩₩	₩₩₩₩ ||	₩₩ |||	||||
DJ	|||	||	|||	₩₩ ||	₩₩₩₩₩	₩₩ ||||	₩₩ |||

2.1 Genre (Uttar Pradesh)

Newspaper	Corruption	Economic	Intl. Politics	Pandemic	Political	Social	Misc.
TOI			||	||||	₩₩ ||	₩₩₩₩	|||	₩₩
DJ	|||			|||	₩₩ ||	₩₩₩₩₩	₩₩ ||||	₩₩ |||

3. Topics Covered

Illustrations published in both the dailies were based on the following issues.

i. Corruption:money in elections, unemployment
ii. Economics: Fall of Indian Rupee, TATA overtakes Air India,
iii. International Politics: China and Sri Lanka, USA and Russia over Ukraine war, Pakistan feeding malnourished Khalistan.
iv. Pandemic: Vaccination drive, vaccination for children, Omicron virus,
v. Politics: Election in Uttar Pradesh, Elections in Punjab, Nomination of Candidates, Kisan protest, Goa elections, Election rallies,
vi. Social: Women empowerment,
vii. Miscellaneous: Djokovic in Australia, Election Commission of India (ECI), social media horoscope

Caricatures Used in Illustrations

i. Narendra Modi, PM India
ii. YogiAdityanath, CM Uttar Pradesh
iii. Putin, President Russia
iv. Priyanka Gandhi, Congress
v. Akhilesh Yadav, President Samajwadi Party.
vi. Swami Prasad Maurya, Politician
vii. Bhagwant Mann, (then) CM face of Punjab
viii. Maharaja of Air India
ix. Lion as Sri Lanka
x. Kangaroo as Australia
xi. Hawk as USA
xii. Shubhash Chandra Bose, founder of Azad Hind Fauj
xiii. Gen. Shah Nawaz Khan, Indian politician and Army officer. (During World War II)
xiv. Navjot Singh Sidhu, (then) CM face of congress
xv. Dragon as China

4. Nomenclature of the Illustrations.

<u>Times of India</u> – TOI publishes a number of illustration and comic strips on regular basis. Due to restricted time of study,researchers have only taken the illustration and not the comic strips such as Dilbert, Hagar, Beetle Bailey which are published regularly. For the sake of this study researchers have taken only two illustrations which are published under the name.

a. Just Like That byAjitNinan
b. Line of No Control by Sandeep Adhwaryu

<u>Dainik Jagran</u>- Dainik Jagran published cartoons on daily basis. During the course of elections, it came up with different series of illustrations under the following names

a. Tarkash by Gayatri
b. Keh Ke rahenge by Madhav Joshi.

Qualitative Analysis

a. **Punjab:** From the data collected by analyzing the illustrations published in both the selected newspapers, researchers came to know that symbolism was the dominant characteristic in almost every illustration. Where the symbolic ECI was presented in one or the other way. Political faces were often exaggerated reflecting the power and wealth they possess. Moreover, the element of analogy is well employed in stating the condition of common man, they are depicted as skinny and in poor condition.Like irony is represented from Subhash Chandra Bose and Shahnawaz talk.
b. **Uttar Pradesh:** From the data collected by analyzing the illustrations published in both the selected newspapers,symbolism is the soul of the illustrations presented. Irony was frequently used along with analogy. Illustration artist have personified the things in the easiest way possible. Exaggeration is used not only to demonstrate public figures but also the contemporary conditions.

Analysis and Findings

From the data collected, researchers analyzed that multiple meanings can be drawn from a single illustration. It depends on the interest and awareness of the readers how well they interpret the message. Illustrations make the best use of symbols. Researchers found that, here illustration artists characterized redsack as China, Hunter as Election Commission of India, Boat as coalition of political parties, different colored Scarf to represent different parties. Slide to depict fall of Indian rupee, Pegasus as violent opposition. All these things give the clear idea what the reality is? An illustration can carry different genres at same time. Therefore, they can be clubbed under socio-economy, socio-polity, economic-corruption etc. It relies on the artist what two ideas should be portrayed. Usual pattern that is observed by the researchers is, illustrations don't have a fixed place in the newspaper. Now-a-days, the placement of illustration is decided by the types of idea and message it carries. For example, if the illustration carried the idea of economy, sports or international politics it is placed on Times Business, Times Sports or Times Global pages of TOI respectively. Similarly,the illustrations related to political news usually make place on the Times Nation page of the newspaper. Illustrations published in Dainik Jagran could be slightly different from point of placement as compared to TOI but they were no different in hitting the same points. Dainik Jagran has reserved a specific place for illustrations to sit. With special reference to the elections researchers come to know that, Dainik Jagran has dedicated an entire page for the assembly elections of the states under the name 'Mahasamar 2022', where they place cartoons on the bottom left of the page hitting hard on elections and pointing towards important issues.Researchers found that newspapers did act as the watchdog of democracy, constantly drawing attention towards the use of foul language by politicians, precautionary negligence during rallies and consensus. The language used in illustrations is easy with a touch of satire and humor. Even the booster dose of Covid-19 is humorously labelled as political. To understand the language, readers must be up to date with the happenings. Sometimes artist employ analogy through verbal sentences.

Researchers have tried to clarify the agenda picked up by both the newspapers to Punjab and Uttar Pradesh and made the analysis by clubbing both the newspaper illustrations. For the same, researchers have studied the data state-wise instead of newspaper-wise. Following is the state-wise analysis of the illustration published in both the newspapers along with some examples of illustrations. Illustration from respective editions are placed just above their analysis

JUST LIKE THAT
AJIT NINAN
TATA
MOTORS
STEEL
HOUSIN
CONSUL
AIG
INDUSTF
POWER
SKY ETC

National Career

LINE OF NO CONTROL
SANDEEP ADHWARYU
GENERAL SHAHNAWAZ WHAT WAS THE MOTTO OF AZAD HIND FAUJ?
'ITTEHAD, ITMAD AUR QUARBANI'
WHAT WOULD WE CALL THESE 75 YEAR CELEBRATIONS ?
JASHN-E-AZADI!

चुनाव 2022
वादे ऐसे करना जो पांच साल में पूरे हों
क्योंकि ये गठबंधन ज्यादा चलने वाला नहीं!
चीन का कर्ज
नया श्रीलंका!

Punjab: Punjabisnorth western state of India with 27 million population (approx.) and literacy rate of 75.84% (as per 2011 census)(Part XII-A, 2014). The total number of registered voters is 2.14 crore.The frequency of illustration and the kind of question raised by them clearly states that every illustration in one way or the other pointed towards the contemporary socio-economic-political conditions. Simple yet effective characters were used to present the clear picture of the scenario. Illustrations depicted each and every step which is important in elections. Right from the social media horoscope illustration, to manifestos till the election rally deadline warning by ECI. The verbal news present on that page give the rough idea of the illustration. Majority of illustration found place on the Times Nation page of TOI, and editorial and op-ed of Dainik Jagran. CM nominees, whether Siddhu, Mann, Yogi or Akhilesh also made way through illustrations. Political turmoil, dramatic allegation and flow of money is quite common during elections. Illustrations magnificently used symbolism and exaggeration to portray these stories. Out of the illustrations published in TOI, 1/4th presented BJP either directly or indirectly. This ratio raised to 1/9th in Dainik Jagran. Increasing cases of Omicron was the second most important issue in illustrations. Labelling and thought bubbles have made the picture bit bright. Rather wasting time in interpreting the illustrations, the text directly hits the bull's eye. In this way the message is simple, clear, direct and effective.

Uttar Pradesh: UP is the Indian state holding the largest population of 190 million and literacy rate of 67.68%. total number of registered voters is 15.02 crore(Part XII-A, 2014). Assembly elections 2022 are portrayed in every other illustration. Out of all, 1/9th of illustration of TOI have thought bubble, which give the clear idea of the situation in a satirical way. Whereas in Dainik Jagran 1/3rd of the illustrations has thought bubbles. Rest illustrations are with(out) label(s), which force readers to derive the meaning by themselves. Metaphors and Pun are employed effectively. 1/9th illustrations of the TOI have directly depicted exaggerated caricatures of the politicians. The frequency rose to 1/7th in Dainik Jagran. More than 50% of the illustration directly portrayed politicians in Dainik Jagran. TOI presented diversity in illustrations, ranging from sports, international politics, Indian economy to omicron variant of Covid-19. Indian economy and sports were less focused in Dainik Jagran, fall of rupee or inflation was not presented from economic point of view but from political view point. ECI was portrayed in the best way possible. Often a male caricature with hunter in hand. The hunter is labelled as ECI, stating the power. Readers can easily identify the caricature of political figures; they wear traditional Indian dress-Kurta-Pajama with a Nehru cap and waist coat. The color of the cap or the coat gives the clear view of the party they belong to. It has been observed by the researchers that instead of cap and coat, scarf characterizes the current dominating political party.

Conclusion and Limitation

From all the data collected and analyzed researchers can conclude that illustrations play an importantrole in setting thewind for election 2022. If not, there would not have been series of illustrations depicting the election process. Illustration artistunderstand their role and responsibility as seriously as reporter and other members associated with newspaper do. Answering the question of agenda setting through illustrations, it can be stated that artist could have focused on some serious social issues that were to be highlighted during these elections. Drug addiction, Kisan protest, safety, basic amenities to name a few. Whereas, in Uttar Pradesh employment, life security, and better health institutions could be highlighted by the artists. Rather than focusing on socio-political economy, majority illustrations focused on prevailing political-economy situations. Illustrations to a great extent were successful in setting the political agenda along with economic. The placement of illustration leaves a huge impact on the viewer. This reasonillustrations are usually placed on the bottom-left of the newspaper can be the two prototype scan paths; one is conventional and the other is perceptual.Dainik Jagran fits well to the conventional order as its all the illustrations are placed on the left bottom of the spread. But the researchers noticed that TOI follows the perceptual order rather than conventional. The placement of illustrations varies and depends upon the topic. The illustrations were able to present the scenario just before the elections. Due to limited time and resources the researchers have restricted theirdata collection to English and Hindi national dailies.

References

[1]Gupta, V. S., &Aggrawal, V. (2001). *Handbook of Journalism and Mass Communication*. Concept Publishing Co.

[2]Paivio, A., &Csapo, K. (1972). Picture superiority in free recall: Imagery or dual coding. *Lund University Cognitive Sciences*. https://doi.org/1972

[3] Brainly.in/questions accessed on 23/09/2022

[4]Sani, I., Abdullah, M. H., Abdullah, F. S., & Ali, A. M. (2012). Political Cartoon as a Vehicle of Setting Social Agenda: The Newspaper Exapmle. *Asian Social Science*. https://doi.org/10.5539/ass.v8n6p156

[5] Kuipers, G. (2011). The Politics of Humor in the Public Sphere: Cartoons Power and Modernity in the first Transnational humor scandal. *European Journal of Cultural Studies*. https://doi.org/2011

[6] Holmberg , N. (2004). Eye movement patterns and newspaper design factors. An experimental approach. *Lund University Cognitive Sciences*. https://doi.org/2004

[7]Sarina, (2020). *Semiotic Analysis of Political cartoons in English newspapers* [Doctoral Dissertation]

[8](2022). *Office of the Registrar General & Census Commissioner, India. Ministry of Home Affairs, Government of India*. eci.gov.in. https://eci.gov.in/statistical-report/statistical-reports/

[9](2014). *Office of the Registrar General & Census Commissioner, India. Ministry of Home Affairs, Government of India*. CensusIndia.gov.in. https://censusindia.gov.in/nada/index.php/catalog/1002

[10]Kress, G., & van Leeuwen, T. (1996). *Reading images: The grammar of visual design* (1st ed.). London: Routledge.

[11] El Refaie, E. (2003).*Understanding visual metaphor: The example of newspaper cartoons". Visual Communications (pp. 75-95)*. London: Sage Publications.

[12] Edwards, J. L. (1997). *Political cartoons in the 1988 presidential campaign: Image, metaphor, and narrative.* New York: Garland

[13]Hussain, T., & Li, B. (2016). NEWSPAPER CARTOONS AS NATIONAL INTEREST AGENDA SETTING TOOL-EXAMPLES FROM PAKISTAN. *Science International, Lahore.* https://doi.org/2016

[14] Han, J. S. N. (2006). Empire of Comic Visions: Japanese Cartoon Journalism and its Pictorial Statements on Korea, 1876–191. *Japanese Studies.* https://doi.org/10.1080/10371390600986637

CHAPTER SIX

An analysis on the dissemination of cultural hegemony in Tamil films

Shamitha Rajesh

Research Scholar, Department of Visual Communication, College of Science and Humanities,

SRM IST, KTR, Tamilnadu – 603 203 sr9108srmist.edu.in

Dr. S Nelsonmandela

Research supervisor

Abstract

Film is an influential medium that portrays and disseminates several social realities and ideologies amongst the masses. Hegemony is one such ideology portrayed in films that establishes a status quo to the audience. There have been several paradigm shifts in the portrayal of hegemony but it has never come to an end. Hegemony is the dominance of one group over another, often supported by legitimating norms, dominant beliefs, ideas, discourse and knowledge. It describes how cultural and ideological leadership is achieved by social groups through dominance.

This research analyses cultural hegemony in Tamil biographical drama portraying real incidents. It throws light on the dissemination of hegemonic power and establishment of a status quo through the films. As (Robert Burgoyne, 2008) puts it, a biopic is "the act of imaginative recreation that allows the spectator to imagine they are 'witnessing again' the events of the past." But the aesthetic and cultural significance of biopics have remained underexplored. Films portraying the recreation of incidents disseminate ideologies that are not fictitious but ones that have been experienced by people in their real life. This portrayal has established the existence of the status quo in the past.

The theoretical framework used in this study is cultural hegemony conceptualised and popularised by Italian, Marxist philosopher, Antonio Gramsci in the year 1971 in his work, Prison Notebooks. The conceptual framework used for the study is critical discourse analysis framework by Van Dijk. It is a framework that is often associated with studying power relations.

A critical discourse analysis has been done on select scenes portraying hegemony from recreation of real incidents in the biographical drama films. This sample chosen for this study is the Tamil biographical drama film, "Thalaivi" by A L Vijay released in the year 2021 based on the life of Indian actor turned politician, J. Jayalalithaa.This study shows the dissemination of hegemony through biographical drama films which are a recreation of real life incidents from Jayalalithaa's life.

Keywords: Hegemony, Gramsci, Biographical drama, Critical discourse analysis, Film analysis

Introduction

Hegemony is the dominance of one group over another. It is a common-sense making and reinforcement process, through dominant beliefs, ideas, discourse and knowledge. It creates consent amongst the people. Dominance has been a part of the society since civilisation began where one group of people identify themselves to be more powerful than the others and they tend to use that power to show their dominance over the submissive group of people. Hegemony was conceptualised to describe this domination through legitimising dominant beliefs and ideas by Antonio Gramsci, Italian Marxist philosopher.

Power structures and domination has been a subject in several films. Recently man Tamil films have depicted the concept of hegemony faced by several people. For example, *Karnan, Pariyerum Perumal, Mandela, Asuran,* etc. One group identifies themselves to be powerful through the culture that they have been following shaped by social institutions. They take power and control and achieve cultural domination. This belief system is hegemony which hides itself behind cultural texts. Power is exercised and reinforced through cultural texts. The depiction of hegemony in films helps the audience understand the social structure and the belief systems that are legitimized by a dominant group of people in the name of culture.

Hegemony representations in terms of gender is a common concept these days. Films depict the gender inequality and there are many female oriented subjects that are breaking this hegemony and emerging themselves as counter hegemonic films. These films showcase the hegemony existing in the society to rationalize the counter hegemonic conclusions. Understanding this depiction of hegemony in the films, helps us in interpreting the dominant ideas and beliefs that have been shaped as culture in the society today. Women have been marginalized and stereotyped in several films but those representations depict the hegemony faced by them. The society has legitimized a dominant belief that men have to be dominant and the subordination of women is essential to maintain the power structure. This normative ideology is referred as hegemonic masculinity.

This research aims to analyse the depiction of hegemony in Tamil films. Interpreting the hegemonic media texts helps us understand the legitimizing beliefs and ideas that have shaped the society. This research aims to identify and interpret the hegemonic masculinity media text that have created and manufactured consent amongst people that men are dominant in the society. Films are a representation of reality and this analysis aims at creating an understanding for the audience to know the power structure and abuse which is a part of the reality.

Objectives

- To analyse the depiction of hegemony in Tamil films
- To identify and interpret the hegemonic masculinity in the depiction

Review of Literature

Cultural hegemony

Historically, hegemony was a Greek term that denoted the dominance of one state over others in a confederacy. It was redefined by Gramsci in his writings as the formation and organization of consent. Currently, hegemony is used to describe power relations in numerous fields, from literature, education, film and cultural studies to politics, history, and international relations (Ives, 2004). Cultural hegemony refers to domination or rule maintained through ideological or cultural means. Social institutions are normally used to accomplish this by influencing the values, norms, ideas, expectations, and worldviews of the rest of society.

According to Gramsci, a communicator chooses vocabulary and style based on their audience and uses it in a way that they hope will communicate their message effectively or accomplish their goals. There may be a degree of ignoring or disrespecting the people spoken about. It is currently defined as 'stereotyping or othering' people - i.e., asserting differences between 'us' and 'them' by making generalizations. Gramsci's notion of hegemony provides an array of concepts to help investigate notions of 'common sense', 'organic intellectuals', 'subalternity' and 'normative versus spontaneous grammar (Ives, 2004).

Hegemonic masculinity

Hegemony originated with (Gramsci, 1971) is essentially a position of dominance achieved by relative consensus rather than regular force. Hegemonic masculinity refers to the normative ideology that to be a man is to be dominant in society and that the subordination of women is required to maintain such power (Connell, 2005). (Connell, 1987) uses the concept of hegemonic masculinity to identify male attitudes and practices that perpetuate gender inequality, including male dominance over women as well as the power of some men over others (often minority groups). As a means of establishing male dominance through subordination and mistrust of women, men are expected to adhere to a set of prescribed masculine gender roles (Malamuth, 1991). (Smith, 2015) in their work states, sexual aggression perpetration can be better understood by deconstructing the overarching constructs of hegemonic masculinity and masculine gender role stress.

Theoretical Framework

The concept of cultural hegemony refers to the dominance of a ruling/ dominant group over other groups in a society with a range of cultures. By directing normative ideas, values, and beliefs that become the dominant worldview of a society, a dominant group of individuals may have the ability to hold power over social institutions, which impacts the everyday thoughts, expectations, and behaviour of the rest of society. An Italian Marxist philosopher named Antonio Gramsci first proposed the concept. During his imprisonment by Mussolini, Gramsci went further with his widely influential notions of hegemony and manufacture of consent in his work, Prison Notebooks (Gramsci, 1971).

Conceptual Framework

Critical discourse analysis is the conceptual framework used for the study. It is a type of discourse analytical research that examines how social power abuse, dominance, and inequality are enacted, reproduced, and resisted through text and talk (Dijk, 2015). The concept of dominance here refers to the exercise of social power by elites, institutions or groups, resulting in social inequality, including inequalities on the basis of political, cultural, class, ethnic, racial or gender (Dijk, 1993).

Understanding social power and dominance is a crucial presupposition of critical discourse analysis (Dijk, 1993). As hegemony is a political or cultural dominance and critical discourse analysis is the ideal framework to examine dominance and its intricacies, it has been chosen as the conceptual framework for the study. The analysis articulates the point of view, perspectives, principles, and aims, both within the discipline and within society at large.

This analysis used the critical discourse analysis framework by Van Dijk. Critical discourse analysis as (Dijk, 2010) defines it, deals with basic concepts, such as micro vs. macro and power as control. According to Van Dijk, language use, discourse, verbal interaction, and communication belong to the micro level of society. The term power, dominance, and inequality between social groups belong to a macro level of analysis.

Tool

The tool for the study to analyse the depiction of hegemony is as used by (Sobur, 2001). The tool analyses the scene in three structures; macrostructure, microstructure and superstructure. There are 6 observations that use many elements to observe the structure as given in Figure

Structure	Observation	Element
Macrostructure	Thematic	Topic
Superstructure	Schematic	Schema
Microstructure	Semantic	Background, detail, intention, presupposition, nominalisation
	Syntactic	Tenses, coherence, pronouns
	Stylistic	Lexicons
	Rhetorical	Graphics, metaphors, expressions

Figure 3.1

Methodology

The study is done using qualitative analysis. Qualitative research is that which collects and analyses non-numerical data. The qualitative data analysis process consists of identifying implicit and explicit dimensions, structures, and meanings in linguistic and visual material. The qualitative analysis used in this study is critical discourse analysis. Critical discourse analysis is the study of how text and talk in social and political contexts enact, reproduce, and resist social power abuse, dominance, and inequality.

Non-probability sampling is chosen for the study. The sampling technique is purposive sampling. Purposive sampling is chosen because it improves the rigour and reliability of the research by matching the sample to the aims and objectives of the study. One biographical drama film is chosen as a sample to identify and interpret hegemonic masculinity in the depictions of hegemony. A biographical drama film dramatizes and depicts the life of a nonfictional or historical figure. Incidents and events from a character's real life are dramatized and scripted to depict the life of a person in the film. The film chosen for the analysis is *Thalaivii* by *AL Vijay*. Released in the year 2021. The film is a portrayal of *J Jayalalitha*, an Indian actress turned politician. The depictions, dialogues and representations in the film are used to understand how the filmmaker wants to people to know and perceive the story. Depicting the dominance and hegemony that happened a few decades ago in a film is to make the audience know the culture, dominance and power structure which was in the society. The hegemony that has been depicted was rooted several years ago. But understanding the dynamic paradigms of hegemony which has shaped the society today, helps in understanding the paradigm shifts which is important for the audience today.

Thalaivii is a film that depicts *Jayalalitha's* life as an actor turned politician. The protagonist in the film who has played the role depicting *Jayalalitha* is named Jaya. The film follows a non-linear screenplay where the film starts with Jaya entering the legislative assembly hall after winning the election as an opposition party and MTK is the ruling party. Then the story navigates to how she came reached that position starting off as a 16-year-old actress forced to enter the field because of her mother. When the story touches the point where it started, it moves to how she became the chief minister of Tamil Nadu. The story ends with Jaya taking up the position of the chief minister and having a small conversation with the party members which is like a prelude to how she will handle things in the future.

Analysis and Interpretation

4.1 Scene 1

Structure- Macrostructure

Observation- Thematic

Element- MJR is the chief minister of Tamil Nadu who is propagating the mid-day meals scheme implemented by Anna. The scheme is not administered or monitored so the schools that are supposed to run the scheme, take the money and don't give the children good food. They serve stale food and the children don't go to the schools because they are not able to eat the food served.

Looking at this unjust, Jaya goes to the school to meet and ask the in charge why this is happening. The in charge refuses to give her an answer by asking her who she is to question all this. He intimidates her and answers her in a very lethargic and disrespectful manner. He says that no one can ask him questions and she is no one to teach him any morals.

Structure- Macrostructure

Observation-Schematic

The scene emphasises two points. Jaya needs a political status to ask a question even if there is injustice. While talking about her profession, he refers to it as "dancing with MJR in a couple of films" and not acting that throws light on people's understanding of an actress.

Structure-Microstructure

Observation- Semantic

Background detail – Once an in-charge has been appointed for any scheme, people cannot ask any questions on its enforcement or welfare unless they have a position or political status to ask the question. For instance, the first person whose name the in-charge utters and thinks can ask him a question is MJR.

Intention – The system cannot be questioned by anyone until and less they have political power. The scene depicts the understanding the in charge who is a representation of people has of an actress. Though she has stepped her foot into politics, they refer to her as a person who has danced with MJR in a couple of films.

Syntactic

Tenses - In terms of the tense, the conversation happens using dialogues in the present and past tense. The past tense is used to question what has happened and the present tense is to question who Jaya is, to ask this question.

Coherence – Jaya sees the ill-maintained schools and the scheme not implemented well and asks the in charge the right questions, logically arranged, and starts at why the scheme is not implemented well and why the money for the scheme is not used properly. The in-charge reply deviated from the question and focuses on who Jaya is to ask these questions. This shows the lack of coherence in the in-charge dialogue proving the point that he is not concerned about what she asks but all his concern is whether she has the status to ask the question.

Pronouns - The pronoun "you" in Tamil is used in 2 ways. "Nee", and "unaku" are considered less respectful, and "neenga", and "ungalluku" is with respect. Jaya in her dialogue uses the pronoun with respect whereas the in-charge does not use the pronoun with respect while addressing Jaya.

Stylistic

The choice of the words "yaaru" in Tamil which translates to "who" emphasises on the status that one seeks in a person to question the system. The words "danced with MJR in a couple of films" delineate the understanding one has of her professional career, acting. The way he addresses Jaya's career is disrespectful.

Rhetorical

Graphics – The scene is composed with establishment shots at the beginning followed by POV shots during the conversation.

Metaphors – The camera angle is composed in a way where Jaya is placed at a lower level than the in charge to show her inferiority.

Expressions – Jayalalitha remains calm and poised throughout though the in-charge shames her. The in-charge becomes furious once she questions him and expresses a lethargic attitude.

4.2 Scene 2

Structure-Macrostructure

Observation-Thematic

Element- Due to her success in administering the mid-day meals scheme and winning in a constituency where there was a backlash against the party, MJR decides to give Jaya a posting in the party called, propaganda secretary. The party members are offended and disappointed with this decision and they voice it out to MJR. The party members observe Jaya's behaviour after getting the posting. She questions the members who have not contributed to the welfare of the party which is a part of her duty. So the members decide to discuss the consequences they are facing because of her with MJR. The party members ask MJR that how she can get the posting and be given the power to question the members who are seniors in the party.

Structure-Superstructure

Observation-Schematic

The issue with giving Jaya the posting is expressed through the dialogue where the members insist that they do not want to be taught politics by a film actress. Though she succeeds in her political career, the members contemplate her as a film actress whom they think does not deserve to be given a posting or power in the party.

Structure-Microstructure

Observation-Semantic

Background detail – Senior members being accused of not working towards the welfare of the party anger them. They are already anguished that the posting was given to Jaya and now they are even more furious that she is questioning them.

Intention - More than the problem of someone questioning them, the dialogue clarifies that a film actress asking the questions and teaching the members to run politics torments them.

Syntactic

Tenses – The tense predominantly used in the discussion is present tense and past tense. Past tense is used to describe what the members have been going through and present tense to discuss their situation.

Coherence – The problem of who is questioning the members comes into a discussion and is navigated to a simile where the members compare the party to a gun and themselves to the bullets in the gun.

Pronouns – The pronouns used to refer to Jaya are alternating between "ava" and "avangalku" which translates to her in two ways, with respect, and without respect.

Stylistic

The word "cinemakaari" is used to address Jaya, which translates to film actress but is expressed disrespectfully. The party members refer themselves to as "bullets" in a "gun" which is the party.

Rhetorical

Graphics – MJR is practising shooting and the party members enter inside. They stop behind a pillar that leaves a special gap between MJR and the members.

As the part members compare themselves with a bullet and the party with a gun where MJR is visually loading a gun with bullets.

Metaphors – While MJR is practising riffle shooting, he misses his aim the first time. After the talk he has with the members and justifies Jaya as the right bullet in the gun, the aim is shot on point.

Expression – The party members' expression depicts disappointment. MJR expresses that his decision is right through his confidence while he shoots the aim.

4.3 Scene 3

Structure-Macrostructure

Observation-Thematic

Element- Jaya tries to meet the Prime minister of India, Congress leader, Indira Gandhi for an alliance in Delhi, where she waits outside the office and the opposition party members see her and interact with her on what she is doing there.

Structure-Superstructure

Observation--Schematic

"Adimai Penn" roughly translated to an enslaved woman is how the opposition party member addresses her. They ask her what business she has there. She being referred to as an enslaved woman represents the perception people have of her and the question that what she is doing there shows that she is not expected to be seen in high places. The opposition party member asks her to use her mind sharply and much as she uses her words.

Structure- Microstructure

Observation- Semantic

Background details – Her party members do not trust her capabilities which have been depicted in many dialogues before this scene. This scene shows that even the opposition party members think of her as an enslaved woman and a person who does not use her mind.

Intention – The opposition party members perceive her as an enslaved woman and a person who can only talk but not think sharply.

Syntactic

Tenses – Present tense is predominantly used in the dialogue as they are discussing why Jaya is in Delhi in the Prime minister's office.

Coherence – The opposition party member associates the profession she used to practice to define the place she is currently at.

Pronoun – The pronouns are used with respect while addressing Jaya and she also uses the pronouns with respect.

Stylistic

"Adimai Penn" roughly translates to enslaved woman emphasising that she is under control.

Rhetorical

Graphics – The scene comprises of POV shots during the conversation.

Metaphors – The metaphor used in the scene is the word, "Adimai Penn" to indicate that Jaya is an enslaved woman for MJR connecting her professional career and her entry into politics because of MJR.

Expression – Jaya remains calm and poised. The opposition party member who converses with Jaya shows confidence in his attitude and expression.

4.4 Scene 4

Structure-Macrostructure

Observation-Thematic

Element- The party members become jealous of Jaya's success in all her endeavours at the party. Out of jealousy, RNV triggers MJR to take away Jaya's propaganda secretary posting and he does so. RNV comes to meet Jaya at the airport and tells her about this. When RNV informs her, Jaya starts laughing because she understands that he is doing all this out of jealousy. She asks him if they are jealous because being a woman, she has accomplished something that the party members couldn't do. RNV accepts the accusation in a lethargic manner and asks her to leave.

Structure-Superstructure

Observation-Schematic

Jaya expresses that she understands the jealousy they have and accepts it with pride because after all, she is the one who has accomplished and proved herself. She mocks him for behaving this way and asks him if she was sent to Delhi to lose and RNV doesn't deny it. He accepts that he is jealous of her success and wants her to fail.

Structure-Microstructure

Observation-Semantic

Background details – RNV has always expressed his vengeance for Jaya at several points in the film, not just when she entered politics but even when she was an actress and used to act with MJR in his films. He has always been jealous of the rapport she has with MJR and tries to dig a grave for her at every chance possible.

Intention – RNV has expressed his vengeance for Jaya. Out of jealousy, RNV adds fuel to the burning fire of MJR and triggers him against Jaya. Using this small opportunity he had, he takes her posting from her and sends her out of the party.

Syntactic

Tenses – The conversation uses present and past tense where what Jaya has done in the past is described using the past tense and their discussion on the current situation is done using the present tense.

Coherence – Jaya correlates RNV's behaviour in the past and understands his vengeance. She asks him about it and RNV does not deny it.

Pronoun – RNV addresses Jaya with the pronoun, "nee" but Jaya uses the pronoun, "neenga" again throwing light on the respect one has for the other.

Stylistic

The dialogue Jaya says, "You can't accept it if a woman accomplishes something" denotes jealousy and Jaya is aware of it and yet determined to achieve more.

Rhetorical

Graphics – The scene is composed with POV shots during the discussion.

Metaphors – The POV shots are composed at an angle where Jaya is placed at a lower level and the shot is a high-angle shot.

Expression – RNV expresses his anger and jealousy and constantly looks away. He does not deliver the dialogue looking at her face but Jaya remains calm and she laughs at him out of sympathy for all the things he's doing out of jealousy.

4.5 Scene 5

Structure-Macrostructure

Observation-Thematic

Element-The legislative assembly discussion is going to begin. The members of both the ruling and the opposition party are taking their places and Karuna, the head of the ruling party TMK is about to read the financial budget for the period. Jaya stops him and interrogates him on some issues that concern her and her party members. The conversation turns into an argument and one member of Karuna's party interrupts and answers Jaya's question. But instead of giving her the answer, he speaks unparliamentary words offending her. In the course of the argument, he asks the other politicians in Jaya's party, MDMK if they are not ashamed to stand behind a woman and accept her as a leader. This argument initiates violence and the party members attack each other. Jaya who tries to calm them down gets assaulted physically.

Structure-Superstructure

Observation-Schematic

The dialogues in the scene emphasise the status Jaya politically and socially needs to ask questions against any injustice that happens to her. They attack her with unparliamentary words. They indulge in physical violence very easily against Jaya, they assault her and intimidate her by pulling her saree.

The scene also indicates how a politician thinks it is shameful for people to stand behind a woman and support her as a leader.

Structure-Microstructure

Observation-Semantic

Background detail – Concerning the background detail of this scene, MJR had just passed away and Jaya is entering the legislative assembly after winning as the opposition party in the year. Many men in her party already have ego issues against Jaya and TMK members have also expressed their notion of seeing Jaya work for the party in the previous scenarios chronologically.

Intention – Men should be ashamed to accept a woman as their leader. Their dominance is depicted in the pride they hold as men and this intention is made clear when Jaya gives her statement after the assault that she will win in this male chauvinistic society. She substantiates the fact that she is being easily cornered and dominated because it was a male dominant society envious of seeing a woman grow.

Presupposition – A woman needs to have a status to ask questions, she cannot grow politically and socially and she will be stopped beyond a particular point by the people.

Syntactic

Tenses – The argument uses present, past and past continuous tenses predominantly. The interrogation by Jaya is spoken in the past continuous depicting that she and her party members were cornered and continued to be troubled. The dialogues about the past events are spoken in the past tense. The other dialogues are spoken in the present tense.

Coherence – The relevance and movement from one concern to the next are logical in terms of Jaya's dialogues. With regards to the TMK politician's dialogue, the relevance is logical but pronouns used to describe Jaya's character, status and profession are disrespectful and unparliamentary.

Pronouns – Jaya, in her interrogation and argument address the chief minister Karuna with respect. The pronoun "you" in Tamil is used in 2 ways. "Nee", and "unaku" which is considered less respectful and "neenga", "ungalluku" is with respect. In Jaya's dialogue, she addresses them using the pronoun with respect but Karuna's party members talks to her, he uses the pronoun without respect.

Stylistic

The choice of using the words, "ashamed to stand behind a woman and call her a leader" depicts the despise and disrespect they have for seeing a woman at a successful place and the men who support her for it.

Rhetorical

Graphics – The tracking shot is composed at a low level where Jaya walks towards the assembly hall climbing the stairs depicting that she enters the place moving higher. The sequence comprises many POV shots during the dialogue.

Metaphors – The entire argument sequence is composed with POV shots at eye level but after the physical abuse, the shot is composed at an angle slightly higher than usual showing that Jaya is inferior to the person she is conversing with. The people who abuse her are placed on the stairs which is at a higher level and she stands down depicting her intimidation.

Jaya speaks against the injustice that happened to her and after her dialogue, the angle of composition changes and she is placed at a higher level. The shot is covered in a low angle showing that she is becoming a superior person in the scene. She walks majestically towards the camera and her party members follow her, depicting that they are not ashamed as accused by the TMK party member.

Expression – Jaya remains calm and confident when interrogating the Chief Minister but when the politician from TMK speaks ill about her, she expresses her disinclination towards it through her expressions. When she is abused physically, she expresses her pain and misogyny.

4.6 Scene 6

Structure-Macrostructure

Observation-Thematic

Element- The party members are discussing about Jaya and her leadership qualities after an unexpected mishap. They are talking amongst themselves that this is a men's world and men should be the ones who rule. They question themselves on how they have given the party to a woman and they're standing behind her. They target her on how as a woman can't protect herself and that they can't trust her to protect and run the party.

Structure-Superstructure

Observation-Schematic

The idea that they emphasise is that this is a men's world and men should be the ones ruling the world. A woman cannot be seen as a leader. The men should not be standing behind her and supporting her. A woman needs someone to protect her.

Structure-Microstructure

Observation-Semantic

Background details – Previously Jaya was abused physically in the assembly and intimidated by the ruling party MTK's members. After the abuse, Jaya stresses the fact that she is being treated this way by the men because this is a male-chauvinistic society. She is aware of this fact and yet she is determined to accomplish her goals.

Intention – Most of the members in the MTMK party were always having vengeance on Jaya and every time there was a downfall, they used it to target her and intentionally convey that she is incapable because she is a woman.

Syntactic

Tenses – The conversation uses past tense where the members describe the incident that has happened and how they have accepted that.

Coherence – The party members relate a momentary downfall faced by Jaya to her incapabilities she is as a leader because she is a woman.

Pronoun – The members address Jaya as "woman" when they talk about her.

Stylistic

"This is a men's world", a dialogue said by one of the members is a blatant statement expressing hegemony.

Rhetorical

Graphics – Initially audio is heard in the background depicting that people are talking about her behind her back sitting in her place.

Metaphors – The members use the same phrase used by a TMK politician to ask if they are not ashamed to accept Jaya as a leader and stand behind her to show that they are accepting his accusation.

Expression – Jaya remains calm and poised. She does not emotionally react to all the statements they give against her.

Scene 7

Structure-Macrostructure

Observation-Thematic

Element-Jaya becomes the chief minister of Tamil Nadu after winning the elections with a majority. She enters her office for the first time after becoming the chief minister. The party members stand outside her room and discuss how Jaya will run the politics. They say that they are everything in the party and she does not know anything about politics. They also say that they are not afraid of her because they are men and she as a woman cannot do anything to them.

Structure-Superstructure

Observation-Schematic

The dialogues, "What can a woman do to us", and "She is dependent on us" outlines the sexist hegemony and male chauvinistic belief the party members have even after seeing her raise to the level of becoming a chief minister. It emphasises the belief that a woman cannot have political knowledge and she can't do anything though she is in one of the most powerful positions. She is looked down upon as an actress and to describe that profession, the members say that she is the one who dances.

Structure-Microstructure

Observation-Semantic

Background details – Jaya becomes chief minister for the first time. She is considered new to politics. She started off as a film actress and her party members associate that profession though she has entered into politics. Though acting is a profession by itself, the members imply the word "dancer" and not actress as a dancer is looked at more inferiorly than an actress.

Intention – A woman does not have an upper hand in politics and she is dependent on men. Though she has progressed in her career from an actress to a politician, her style of politics will be influenced by how an actress performs, ordered and guided by someone.

Syntactic

Tenses – The tenses used in the conversation are future tense and present tense. The future tense is used to discuss how the party will be run and the present to discuss their intentions and presuppositions.

Coherence – The members associate her acting career with how she will run politics. The simile used to compare her politics is her acting profession where they say they are the directors and she will be the actress who listens to their commands. The word used to describe her as an actress is the one who dances, not an actress.

Pronoun – The members use the pronoun to refer to Jaya and occasionally use the word "woman" to address her.

Stylistic

The members insist on the idea that Jaya is dependent on them for politics and that is expressed through the words "What does she know about politics", and "We are everything". She is still regarded as an actress handling politics where will act and the party members will have the command in their hands which is expressed through the words, "We will say start, camera and action even if she is the one dancing".

Rhetorical

Graphics – The members stand outside her room and have this discussion which indicates that they're talking behind her back.

Metaphors – The members relate the profession she initially started to denote her capabilities even after she moved to a different profession and proved herself politically by winning the state elections.

Expression – The expressions are natural and incidental as the discussion is an informal casual talk between the members.

Findings and Conclusion

The film *Thalaivii* has several scenes that depict hegemony. The dialogues of the men in the film emphasize the fact that Jaya is a woman and a woman cannot be successful in politics. Several scenes depict that a woman needs status to voice out for herself and for society. Jaya and MJR are both actors turned politicians but MJR was never addressed as the one who dances in films whereas Jaya in several places is addressed as a cinema person, the one who dances though she has moved into politics. She is even referred to as an enslaved woman as she was in a profession where she does her work based on orders. Jaya is a well-aware woman knowing that her success being a woman is making the men jealous and they accept it. Jay is always cornered with a demand for political status to voice out anything. The men who support her are humiliated for standing behind and supporting her because she is a woman. She is physically assaulted and she calls out the men telling them that she is aware that they have taken power in their hands because this is a male-chauvinistic world. The men express their male chauvinistic beliefs that this is a man's world and men should rule it with confidence. They even believe that, though Jaya has reached a politically successful point, she will be dependent on them and cannot do anything to them because she is a woman. Based on the analysis, a conclusion is drawn that the scenes and dialogues express dominating standpoints of the characters but particularly it converges at a point that the dominance is because Jaya is a woman. Based on the definition by (Connell, 2005), the film depicts hegemonic masculinity which is the normative ideology that to be a man is to be dominant in society and that the subordination of women is required to maintain such power. Therefore, the characters in the film have expressed hegemonic masculinity against the protagonist of the film, Jaya. This analysis has scrutinized the depiction of hegemony. It has interpreted the representation of hegemonic masculinity and shed light on the depiction.

REFERENCES

- Connell, R. W., & Messerschmidt, J. W. (2005). Hegemonic masculinity rethinking the concept. In *Gender and Society* (Vol. 19, Issue 6, pp. 829–859). SAGE Publications Inc. https://doi.org/10.1177/0891243205278639
- Djamila, A. (n.d.). *Critical Discourse Analysis*
- Donaldson, M. (1993). *Recommended Citation Recommended Citation Donaldson, Mike, What Is Hegemonic Masculinity?*
- Ives, P. (2004). *Language and hegemony in Gramsci.* Pluto Press.
- Jewkes, R., Morrell, R., Hearn, J., Lundqvist, E., Blackbeard, D., Lindegger, G., Quayle, M., Sikweyiya, Y., & Gottzén, L. (2015). Hegemonic masculinity: combining theory and practice in gender interventions. *Culture, Health and Sexuality, 17,* 112–127. https://doi.org/10.1080/13691058.2015.1085094
- Kunsey, I. (n.d.). *Representations of Women in Popular Film: A Study of Gender Inequality in 2018.*
- Lears, T. J. J. (n.d.). *The Concept of Cultural Hegemony: Problems and Possibilities.*
- Li, Q. (2016). Theoretical Framework of Critical Discourse Analysis. *Studies in Literature and Language, 13*(5), 36. https://doi.org/10.3968/9066
- Litowitz, D. (2000). Gramsci, Hegemony, and the Law Recommended Citation Gramsci, Hegemony, and the Law. In *BYU Law Review* (Vol. 515).
- Mouffe, C. (n.d.). *5 Hegemony and ideology in Gramsci.*
- Pradeep, K. (n.d.). Analysing Tamil Films with Critical Discourse Analysis Approach. *International Journal of Linguistics and Computational Applications (IJLCA) (Print), 3*(3).
- Rodrigues, S. (n.d.). *Routledge Critical Thinkers*
- Smith, R. M., Parrott, D. J., & Tharp, A. T. (2015). Deconstructing hegemonic masculinity: The roles of antifemininity, subordination to

women, and sexual dominance in men's perpetration of sexual aggression. *Psychology of Men and Masculinity, 16*(2), 160–169. https://doi.org/10.1037/a0035956

- Sobur, A. (2001). *Analisis teks media: Suatu pengantar untuk analisis wacana, analisis semiotik dan analisis framing.* Bandung, Indonesia: PT. Remaja Rosdakarya
- Tannen, D., Hamilton, H. E., & Schiffrin, D. (n.d.). *Discourse Analysis Second Edition Volume I.*
- Tavakoli, H., Tabrizi, H. H., & Ling, E. (2014). Critical Discourse Analysis Scrutinizing Ideologically-Driven Models. In *& Trans* (Vol. 71). https://www.researchgate.net/publication/329687214
- Uchendu, O. N. (n.d.). *Gender Representation In Nollywood Video Film Culture.*
- Ulinnuha, R., Udasmoro, W., & Wijaya, Y. (2013). Critical discourse analysis: theory and method in social and literary framework. In *Indonesian Journal of Applied Linguistics* (Vol. 2, Issue 2).
- van Dijk, T. A. (1993). Principles of critical discourse analysis. *Discourse & Society,* 4(2), 249–283. https://doi.org/10.1177/ 0957926593004002006
- Van Dijk, Teun A. "Discourse analysis as ideology analysis." *Language & peace.* Routledge, 2005. 41-58.

CHAPTER SEVEN

An Analysis on Understanding Youth's Favorite Online Games and Gaming Literacy

Mr. Vijayaraj. M[1] Dr. Nelsonmandela.S[2]

[1]Research Scholar,
Department of Visual Communication
Faculty of Science and Humanities
SRM Institute of Science and Technology
vm3913@srmist.edu.in
[2]Assistant Professor
Department of Visual Communication
Faculty of Science and Humanities
SRM Institute of Science and Technology
nelsonms@srmist.edu.in

Abstract

The Internet has changed many things in daily activities. And that is reflected in the playing style of children and youth. Due to the development of technologies and the increased use of the Internet, online connectivity and social media usage has created a huge impact. Due to urban development and apartment culture, children are less likely to play outside and engage in computer and mobile games. Also, the impact of the Covid-19 lockdown has paralyzed people at home. This has helped and increased the pea group combining online games and virtual reality games. Through play, children feel connected to their friends and build paddles just like in the real world. Voice chat technology has made young people engage in online games. This is because they can interact with their peer groups to complete the task of the game which gives them real-world experience. Teenagers are interested in playing various online games and games with different approaches and rules. The main objective of this study is how much teenagers know about online games and what kind of special features they like about online games. is to find out. And what kind of games are today's youth's playing the most? The main objective of the study is to find out its characteristics. Randomly 162youth's are selected as a sample and data are obtained through a questionnaire in the survey method through which the required details can be found.

Keywords: Online Games, Youth's, Covid-19, Reality games, Paddles

Introduction

Online video games are an important source of entertainment and general entertainment. The popularity of video games has grown tremendously over time. Across cultures around the world. These Internet-based information and communication technologies have led to the creation of new types of communities and cultural communication practices (Wilson & Peterson, 2002). Video games helped create a virtual world. A self-constructed and autonomous view of structures and processes not explained by the real world (Boellstorf, 2008). Virtual worlds are immersive. And because they look and sound like the real thing, players must be able to manipulate the world-like elements to experience the world and thus the degree of existence (Golub, 2010).

Also, this emerging culture of video Games can be seen to be popular among the youth and young adults in Tamil Nadu The amount of time they spend in the virtual world is very high. Time they spend with real people in the real world. This is somewhat worrisome because a child's social and cultural development is affected by activities. They engage with computer and smartphone screens. (Palmer, 2006). As a result, video games have always been a controversial topic around the world. Recently, one of the most popular online video games, 'PlayerUnknown's Battlegrounds' (PUBG), has been banned in some countries and is facing a possible ban. Due to the alleged crime in many parts of India (Mamun & Griffiths, 2019). Negative impact on education, health and psychology of young people (Sekos, 2019). For the same reasons, in Tamil Nadu also the State Govt The process of banning the game started in September 2020.

Outrage from parents and many civil societies. Amid these controversies, the youth and young adults continue to play online video games as a pastime Sometimes addictive. The present study is an attempt to understand the players' subjective perceptions of how the younger generation perceives video as a cultural representation and how games are growing in popularity among young people in Tamil communities. There are many influences and effects on the players.

Review of Literature

(Pampi, 2021)The study is an attempt to understand players' perceptions and reasons for spending hours playing it. This article also examines the factors responsible for the development. The impact of excessive gaming on the lives of gamers as a whole. found in this study. Data has been collected from important samples through questionnaire. The popularity of a particular sport. It is an extra realistic gaming experience that online games offer, which is very addictive. Players are also revealed to be fundamentally unlike some areas of socially accepted entertainment in Arunachal Pradesh.This article focuses on insights about players.

(Antonius J. van Rooij, 2010)Objectives to provide empirical data-based identification of a group of addicted online gamers. Repeat the design A cross-sectional study was conducted in 2008 and 2009. Schools in the Netherlands. Participants were two large samples of Dutch schoolchildren (aged 13–16 years). Measures were compulsive Internet use volume, weekly hours of online gaming, and psychological variables. Findings This study confirms the existence of a small group of addicted online gamers (3%), which is about 1.5%. Among all children aged 13–16 years in the Netherlands. Although these gamers report relationship problems, such as addiction Poor psychosocial health was less common. Results are indicative of a small group Support effort to develop and validate questionnaire scales aimed at measuring the phenomenon of addicted online gamers

Methodology

The study is being conducted among the students ofthe SRM Institute of science and technology, Kattankulathurcampus, which was very close to the capital city of Tamil Nadu. The main reason for choosing this campus is because the parents and students come here from different regions of the country. Also, this study aims to explore popular video game culture among youth. Compared to other places in Tamil Nadu, Chengalpattu and Chennai have the largest number of schools, colleges, and universities, so the target population is large. The sample of the study was selected using a purposive random sampling method where only those who played video games were considered. The study is a quantitative survey method in its approach, and data was collected using questionnaires. Focusing on the main objectives of the study, an online questionnaire consisting of both closed-ended and open-ended was constructed. The questionnaire was distributed online to the respondents by responding on Facebook, Instagram, and WhatsApp groups. Share the link with people they know who are playing online games. In total, 162 respondents filled out the questionnaire, of which 72% were males and 28% were females. The sample population of this study consisted mostly of high school and college students and young adults who admitted to being sporty. Respondents are mostly between 17-21 years of age.

Discussion and analysis

Sample distribution regarding age

The focused random sampling technique used for this study contains the sample distribution of more than 160 respondents and the data collected through the google form in 2022. Because the data was collected only from the age group between the last phase of youth's (17) to starting phase of adulthood (21) for a better understanding of the influence of online gaming addiction and to know about the literacy of online games among college students who regularly play online games in their day-to-day life. This shows the respondents were valid for the research to understand the impact of online gaming on the student's life cycle.

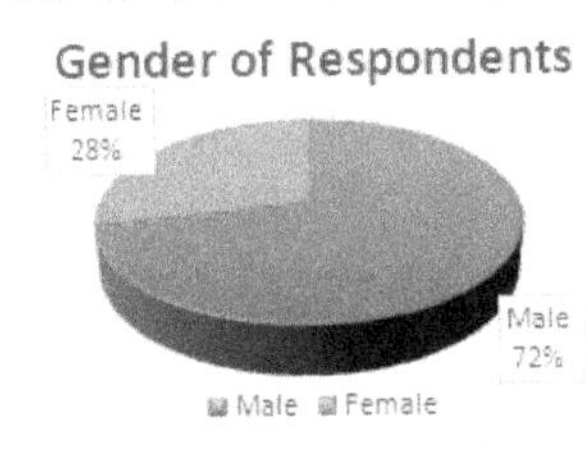

Fig. 1.1

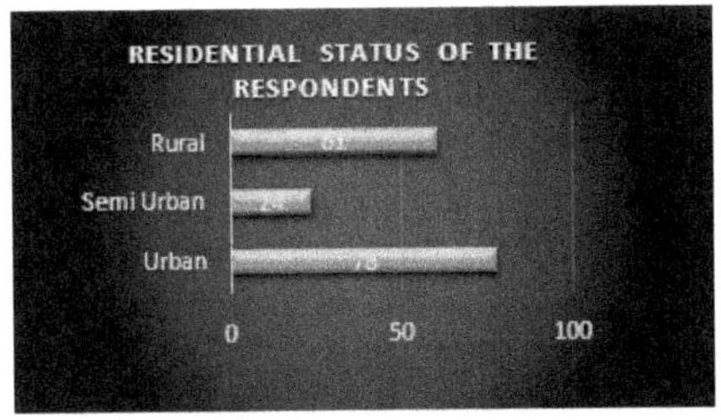

Fig. 1.2

Enter Caption

Fig 1.1, shows that more than 70 percent of the respondents were male and nearly 30 percent of the respondents were female. This shows that apart from the social media fever most youngsters are engaging themselves with online gaming to manage their boredom. The data shows that **(Fig 1.2)** more than 100 participants belong to the Urban and semi-urban areas which provides the scope for the students to know more about the online games for the social connectivity and lack of outside atmosphere create an addiction to the particular popular culture. Apartment-based lifestyle and the Covid-19 lockdown created a huge impact on the lifestyle change and playing pattern change of the Ganz people. Interestingly, more than 61 students belong to rural areas playing online games. This result shows how the globalization process, the intervention of Jio telecom service, and the digital India process create awareness and impact in the rural area people. All the respondents were aware of the online game and they spent regularly few hours a day playing those games for their relief.

Fig 1.3: The graphical figure was about the response detail to the question 'How you are aware of online games?'

Fig. 1.3

Fig 1.3, shows that 33.7 percent of the respondents get to know about the updates and the new release of the online games through the peer group. Also, they mentioned that they were aware of online games through their friends in most cases. Also, more than 80 respondents that are, 50.6 percent of the students mentioned that they get to know the regular updates about the online games through social media peer groups and other meme pages, and official sites of the game providers. This shows the social connectivity of these people through the online platforms provide the needed information for the online game uses. Also, because of the online classes taken during the pandemic made the Ganz people socially connect for every bit of the information. This result shows that technology natives spend more time on social media for relief and the social connection parameters. Only 9 percent of the respondents said that they were aware of the online games and new lunches through the advertisements. Another 6 percent of the respondents said that they were aware of the online games through family members of the same age group.

Fig 1.4: The graphical figure shows the audience preferred genre of online games.

The graphical figure **(Fig 1.4)**, shows that more than 31 percent of the respondents prefer Action games as their favorite. 24 percent of the respondents reacted to adventure-type games as their preferred genre for playing online for a better audience experience. More than 17 percent of the respondents mentioned battle royal games as their favourite genre type. Nearly 14 percent of the audience played arcade games in their free time for better engagement and a peaceful experience. Another 14 percent of the respondents said that they prefer Massive multiple online role-playing games because of the better graphics and engaging factors.

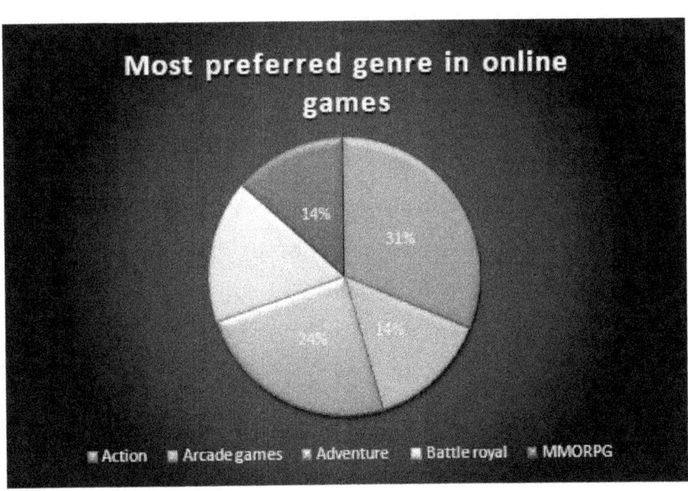

Fig. 1.4

From the above figure, we could easily conclude that Action and adventure-type games were the most preferred genre of the current generation audience. Also, they like multiplayer role-play games for a better user experience.

Also, they mentioned Valorant, Call of duty, free fire, PUBG, Jungle adventure, Modern warfare, and Adventure Escape mysteries were the notable online games played by the respondents. More than 100 respondents said that they use mobile phones for playing online games, and 25 responded that they use computers and laptops for playing online games. Apart from this other respondent mentioned that they use gaming machines like play station and Xbox for playing online games. 34.5 percent of the respondents play online games at regular intervals each day. 31.5 percent of the respondents mentioned that they play the games very often. Others responded that they play online games with the urge, for every update they wait for a reasonable duration and they access games whenever they felt free. Most of the respondents spend more than 10 hours a week playing online games, which made them addicted to those games. Because of the continuous activity of the respondents by playing online games, they often feel physical pain and eye-related issues. More than 70 percent of the respondents mentioned that they felt that kind of physical pain during and after playing online games.

More than 20 percent of the respondents mentioned that they spend money on online games for the user experience and premium offered by the gaming company. To showcase their dominance and connected with the peer group some of the respondents spent money on purchasing the elite gift vouchers and other offers provided in the game. Most of the students spend nearly 3 thousand to 5 thousand per month on online games for elite vouchers and other customized costumes in role-playing games. More than 50 percent of the respondents said that they could feel some behavior change after the continuous playing of the online game. Even though 48 percent of the respondents said that they never experience any behavior change because of the online games.

Fig 1.5: The graphical figure shows the audience response related to the purpose of playing online games.

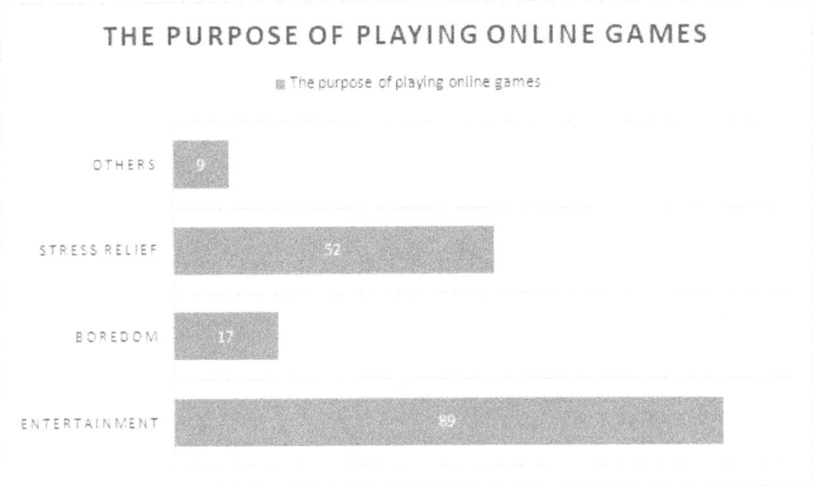

Fig. 1.5

Fig 1.5, clearly shows that most of the respondents play online games for entertainment purposes. Nearly 54 percent of the respondents mentioned that they use online games for entertainment purposes and to escape from the reality. 32 percent of the respondents mentioned that they use online games for stress relief factor. Get out from the routine stress and engage with the peer group most of the respondents use online games and role-play multiplayer games. Nearly 10 percent of the students said that they use online games for relief from boredom, which is caused by routine activity. Only 9 respondents mentioned those other parameters also responsible for playing the online games like regular interest and curiosity, offers provided by the gaming sites for the regular login and completing the tasks. Peer group completion for social connectivity also plays a major role in the regular use of online games. The virtual creation of a new world shown by online games attracts most of the respondents to regularly play those games for real-world satisfaction.

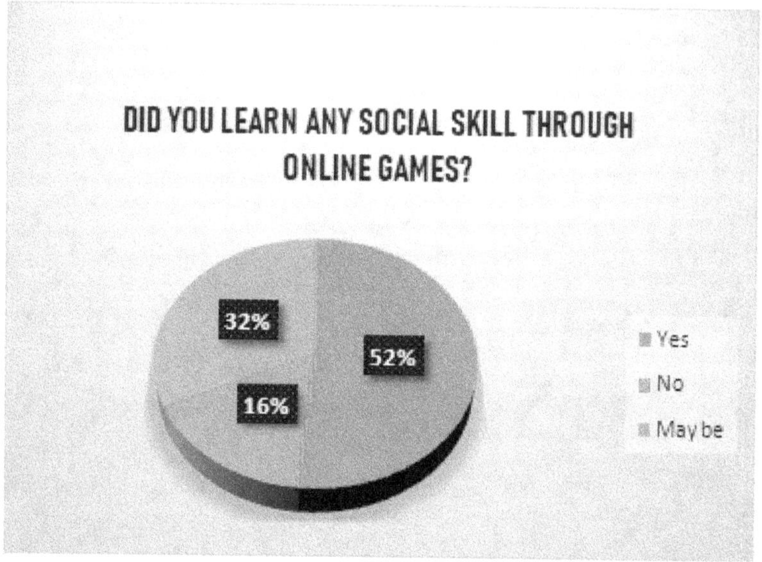

Fig. 1.6

Fig 1.6: The graphical figure shows the audience response related to the purpose of playing online games.

Fig 1.6, shows more than 80 percent of the respondents mentioned that they could learn some social skills and literacy through online games. Some of them mentioned that their language was improved and learned a few new words through the online role-playing games. Respondents mentioned further that, they learned the rules of games like football, and tennis through online games. Also, few said that because of online social games they make new friends from different parts of the world because of their only mutual interest in playing games. Only 16 percent of the respondents refuged that they never learned any new skill or social connecting habit from the games. Also, they mentioned that they only play games with their peer group not with any strangers and they play games for entertainment satisfaction. So that they never put any effect on improvising their skills in any aspect.

Through the survey, the researchers could conclude that by playing online games the focused group faced some negative impacts and they felt addicted to the games. Nearly 75 percent of the respondents mentioned that because of playing the online game they could feel the enormous impact in the sense of the physical, mental, and psychological aspects. Also, more than 80 percent of the respondents reacted that they were aware about they were addicted to online games. Only less than 25 percent of the respondent refused to accept the addiction level and other impact factors caused because of the online games. They might still not be aware of or experienced those factors.

Conclusion

The result of the studyclearly shows that all Gen Z students have the access to digital technologies, even during school times. For the online class purpose current students under the age group of 17 to 21, hold their personal handset or laptop, which provides space and access opportunities for playing online games. That made most of the focus group addicted to the online games and they played a different kind of massively multiplayer online role-playing games. More than 75 percent of the respondents of the focus group agreed that they were addicted to online games and they felt some mental, or psychological impact on their regular routine. The metaverse development might have a huge impact on those people who spend more time playing games. So, this area should be addressed now itself for the betterment of the upcoming generation of India. If the popular culture of playing online games became a routine it might affect the educational pattern and impact the behaviors of the upcoming youngsters. Also, this study was conducted only with a minimal population, if the numbers might increase the result also gets influenced. The researcher suggested that understanding the urge to play online games, and the social connection aspect of the students should be studied in wider form for further study. Also, to understand or measure the addiction level and behavior changes among the focus group.

References

- Müller, K. W., Janikian, M., Dreier, M., Wölfling, K., Beutel, M. E., Tzavara, C., Richardson, C., &Tsitsika, A. (2015). Regular gaming behavior and internet gaming disorder in European adolescents: results from a cross-national representative survey of prevalence, predictors, and psychopathological correlates. *European Child and Adolescent Psychiatry*, 24(5), 565–574. https://doi.org/10.1007/s00787-014-0611-2

- Apperley, T., & Walsh, C. (2012). What digital games and literacy have in common: A heuristic for understanding pupils' gaming literacy. *Literacy*, *46*(3), 115–122. https://doi.org/10.1111/j.1741-4369.2012.00668.x

- Author, L., Gerber, H. R., & Price, D. P. (2011). Twenty-First-Century Adolescents, Writing, and New Media: Meeting the Challenge with Game Controllers. In *Source: The English Journal* (Vol. 101, Issue 2).

- Leander, K. M., &Lovvorn, J. F. (2006). Literacy Networks: Following the Circulation of Texts, Bodies, and Objects in the Schooling and Online Gaming of One Youth. In *COGNITION AND INSTRUCTION* (Vol. 24, Issue 3).

- Badrinarayanan, V. A., Sierra, J. J., & Martin, K. M. (2015). A dual identification framework of online multiplayer video games: The case of massively multiplayer online role playing games (MMORPGs). *Journal of Business Research*, *68*(5), 1045–1052. https://doi.org/10.1016/j.jbusres.2014.10.006

- Felszeghy, S., Pasonen-Seppänen, S., Koskela, A., Nieminen, P., Härkönen, K., Paldanius, K. M. A., Gabbouj, S., Ketola, K., Hiltunen, M., Lundin, M., Haapaniemi, T., Sointu, E., Bauman, E. B., Gilbert, G. E., Morton, D., &Mahonen, A. (2019). Using online game-based platforms to improve student performance and engagement in histology teaching. *BMC Medical Education*, *19*(1). https://doi.org/10.1186/s12909-019-1701-0

- Procci, K., Bohnsack, J., & Bowers, C. (2011). LNCS 6774 - Patterns of Gaming Preferences and Serious Game Effectiveness. In *LNCS* (Vol. 6774).

- Hanghøj, T., Kabel, K., & Jensen, S. H. (2022). DIGITAL GAMES, LITERACY AND LANGUAGE LEARNING IN L1 AND L2. *L1 Educational Studies in Language and Literature, Speciall Issue*. https://doi.org/10.21248/l1esll.2022.22.2.363

- Beavis, C., Apperley, T., Bradford, C., O'Mara, J., & Walsh, C. (2009). Literacy in the digital age: Learning from computer games. *English in Education*, *43*(2), 162–175. https://doi.org/10.1111/j.1754-8845.2009.01035.x

- Rosenberg, K., Liu, S., Gathegi, J., & Watson, R. (2011). *Gaming Literacy: Construct Validation and Scale Construction*.

- Paulus, F. W., Ohmann, S., von Gontard, A., &Popow, C. (2018). Internet gaming disorder in children and adolescents: a systematic review. In

Developmental Medicine and Child Neurology (Vol. 60, Issue 7, pp. 645–659). Blackwell Publishing Ltd. https://doi.org/10.1111/dmcn.13754

- Kökönyei, G., Kocsel, N., Király, O., Griffiths, M. D., Galambos, A., Magi, A., Paksi, B., &Demetrovics, Z. (2019). The role of cognitive emotion regulation strategies in problem gaming among adolescents: A nationally representative survey study. *Frontiers in Psychiatry, 10*(APR). https://doi.org/10.3389/fpsyt.2019.00273
- Seok, H. J., Lee, J. M., Park, C. Y., & Park, J. Y. (2018). Understanding internet gaming addiction among South Korean adolescents through photovoice. *Children and Youth Services Review, 94,* 35–42. https://doi.org/10.1016/j.childyouth.2018.09.009
- Pampi, M., & Asghar, M. (2021). A Blur Line Between Hobby and Addiction: Online Video Gaming Among the Youth of Arunachal Pradesh. *Oriental Anthropologist, 21*(1), 116–124. https://doi.org/10.1177/0972558X21994249
- van Rooij, A. J., Schoenmakers, T. M., Vermulst, A. A., van den Eijnden, R. J. J. M., & van de Mheen, D. (2011). Online video game addiction: Identification of addicted adolescent gamers. *Addiction, 106*(1), 205–212. https://doi.org/10.1111/j.1360-0443.2010.03104.x
- Kuss, D. J., & Griffiths, M. D. (2012). Online gaming addiction in children and adolescents: A review of empirical research. In *Journal of Behavioral Addictions* (Vol. 1, Issue 1, pp. 3–22). AkademiaiKiado Rt. https://doi.org/10.1556/JBA.1.2012.1.1

CHAPTER EIGHT

Evolution of Popular Fiction in India

Ganta Nikhil Kumar
PhD Research Scholar
Department of English,
Dr. Babasaheb Ambedkar Technological University, Lonere-Raigad,
Maharashtra, India
gnikhil15@gmail.com

Abstract

Indian Popular fiction has an ever growing readership in India and its readers have a voracious appetite for content and seem to have an unquenchable thirst for fiction. Although its inception was bumpy with its initial imitative awkwardness which suffered an identity crisis, it later grew leaps and bounds with the current market estimate around 739 billion rupees. The present article briefly examines the evolution of popular fiction from 19th to 21st century and its transformation from being a colonial child to its hybridization and Indianisation.

Keywords: Popular fiction, Evolution, Hybridization, Globalization

Introduction

Indian English literature says M.K. Naik is a byproduct of the encounter between colonial Britain and chaotic India (Naik, 2008). A language which was just a pidgin soon became the *lingua franca*. Seldom did the British realize that English would be a global language. The Indian English literature is also called as Indo-Anglian literature because it is a mixture of standard English spoken by Britain and the native English used by Indians. This amalgamation created a new variety of English literature. This is not be confused with another body of writing which is translations of original work written in native languages. Translations from the Indian languages into English cannot form part of Indian English literature, except when they are creative translations by the authors themselves.

The British had come to India in the beginnings of the 17th century as East India Company. Their primary goal was commerce and not conquest. But later on they have filled in the loose void left by the Mughals and became the ruling power in India. This for them became an opportunity to spread their language and arrangements were made to introduce English language and reject the native *Gurukool* system. Macaulay believed native Indian languages as outdated and professed the superiority of English language in his infamous Minute (Macaulay, 1835). This Minute was responsible for the establishment of the need for Indian natives to receive an English education.

Macaulay had no idea that his 'English Education Act of 1835', a colonial endeavour to appropriate and subsume our languages and literatures would result in the resurgence of the same by the way of the 'Indian Renaissance'. The gradual spread of English education and Western ideas brought forth a band of earnest Indians who drank deep at the fountain of European learning. The Indian renaissance was less like the European one and more like the Celtic movement in Ireland. It was 'the attempt of a reawakened national spirit to find a new impulse of self-expression which shall give the spiritual force for a great reshaping and rebuilding.'(Aurobindo, 2002)

Pulp Fiction and Popular Fiction

There is a distinction between popular fiction and pulp fiction. Pulp fiction is as the name indicates made with 'pulp' which means fiction printed on cheap kind of paper i.e. from pulp (made from rags and wastepaper). They usually feature semi-clad women, speeding cars and haunted mansions. These kinds of fiction are either translated into languages like Hindi, Urdu, Tamil, Bangla and Marathi or written originally in such languages (Khair, 2008). Whereas popular fiction belongs to a work of fiction that has proved to be popular with wide range of audiences. What is a popular fiction novel? It is important to discover and classify the novels and writers. Keeping in mind the concept of readership, does an average reader of Indian English fiction has this sense of aesthetic value? If we look at history there was always a conflict between traditional mainstream Literature and popular fiction. Popular fiction appeased the masses while the mainstream literature was pursued by the elite classes or the aristocracy only. There exists a narrow boundary between these two types. Often times we can see the trend of a popular fiction becoming a classic and attaining the status of mainstream literature. In this context can we assume Indian English literature which is again a branch of English literature be considered mainstream literature. The complexity between the novels published in the category of Indian English literature also differs. For example the novel *God of Small Things* (1997) by Arundhati Roy comes in the category of literary. Whereas *Five Point Someone* (2004) by Chetan Bhagat comes in the category of popular fiction. The latter has high readership and reach within India while the formal has poetical prowess and holds a significant role in the west. This is opposite from <u>literary fiction,</u> which tends to be more non-academic, does not invite analysis and has a more narrow market among the scholarly. The common factors agreed upon by most though are that popular fiction is an easy read, is formulaic, entertaining and escapist, and targets the mass market with the lowest common literary denominator.

Inception of Popular Fiction in India

At the inception writers like Bankim Chandra Chatterjee, Toru Dutt, Lal Behari Dey and K.K. Lahiri among a few others qualify to be in popular literature. The development of printing press, establishment of universities and increasing literacy levels were responsible for more Indians reading English fiction written by Indians. Thus the English readership in India grew. The fictional work during this period was imitative and experimental. A standard form which was suitable for Indian readers had not been developed yet. The language Indian writers used was the 'language of the colonizers' (Chawla, 2022, p.24)). English for us then was an adopted language which did not have an indigenous feel and touch to it. Such experimentations can be seen in the works such as *Rajmohan's Wife* (1864) by Bankim Chandra Chatterjee and others. The Indians had found a new voice in an alien tongue and their expression was to become a global one because of the International readership. But during this period there were only few who could handle the English language with its intricate fluency.

The Indian English novel, says Amit Chaudhuri, is a "colonial child", a "cross pollination of language, race and art" (Chawla, 2022, p22). This amalgamation of two languages can be seen in the next wave of writers who firmly established Indian English as the *lingua franca*. The famed trio are Raja Rao, Mulk Raj Anand and R.K. Narayan. They are the stalwarts who have covered a vast area of subjects relating to India and its society. Raja rao's novels consists an 'epic breadth of vision, metaphysical depth, a symbolical richness, a lyrical fervour and essential Indianness of style'. This Indianess is what differentiates an Indian novel from its western counterparts. There are certain aspects in an Indian novel which are near and dear only to the hearts of the Indians whether it may be about the society, language, culture or socio-political environment. R.K. Narayan in his works turns his gaze towards Indian villages and the rural experience. His famous fictional town of Malgudi and its characters remain a nostalgic memory and bring a certain joy in the readers who cherish the brilliance of his writings. Mulk Raj Anand exposed the blunt realities of caste and social exploitation in his ground breaking novels. His novel *Untouchables* (1935) deals with the evil of untouchabililty, injustice, humiliations, and degradation faced by the marginalized sections which is even visible and conspicuous in modern Indian society.

Mid-Phase

Indian Independence was a high period for Indian Writing in English. People were imbued with a wave of Nationalistic spirits. 200 years of British rule and its imperial tyranny had taken a toll on the Indian psyche. When Indians were rebelling against the British rule, the effect also manifested in the novels written during those period. Novels of Manohar Malgoankar give us a glimpse into the mindset of people before Independence. His style was no longer the Queen's language. It had its own Indian overtones to its style and form. The initial imitative awkwardness was no longer present and the writers wrote boldly and confidently. Fiction during this period was imbued with the spirit of social reform and Nationalism which uncovered the hypocrisies and shams of Indian society. Just following the Independence India faced a huge crisis of partition where India got divided into two countries. Partition novels where especially very popular during this period. Novels of Khushwant Singh and Salman Rushidie explore the theme of partition and its effects. *Train to Pakistan* (1956)portrays the horrors of partition which divided nations and families across the border. Salman Rushidie's *Midnight's Children* (1981)was an important marker in Indian Literature in English. It was a decisive shift in language and content. We can see the use of 'Hybridised English' and an experimentation of a style called 'Magic Realism'. The novel explained the process of building the nation- from the British colonial rule to Independence including the partition.

Then comes the phase of writers who wrote about contemporary Indian society of the later part of 20th century. This includes the phase of India and its development past 25 years and beyond after India's Independence. Writers like Rohinton Mistry wrote about the socio-economic development as well as the political emergencies of 70's. The theme of popular fiction was no longer rural and it had already shifted to the urban landscape. They began to write about the insider's perspective into the sordid upper class stilettoed society with a potent mix of sex, money and intrigue. Shobha De offers us the changing structure of society, an aspirational social mobility and an Indianized middle class version of the American Dream. Her stories mainly include the tales of material success and fame in a world of intrigue and opportunities. The novels during this period consisted of indigenized English which included much code mixing and code switching.

Indian Popular fiction in the 21st century

The stage has been set for the upcoming metro-based popular cosmopolitan fiction. The 21st century has been a golden period for the sale of Indian Writing in English. The sale of the Indian English Fiction had seen an unprecedented rise. The campus novels of Chetan Bhagat were a massive hit and he was according to *The New York Times* 'the best selling English language novelist in India's History'. With clever strategy and marketing he was able to appease to a wide range of audiences. He appealed to the young middle class, spoke their language with their distinctive lingo which resonated with their aspirations. The style and prose of his language was simple and clearly demarcated from those of literary writers like Arundhathi Roy and Salman Rushidie. The easiness of prose increased the likeability of readers who are not acquainted with high fiction. His novels were so successful that they were even made into featured Bollywood films. His novel *The 3 Mistakes of my Life* (2008) sold 4,20,000 copies while *Five Point Someone (2004)* had sales of more than 7,00,000 copies in India. The common theme behind his campus novels was the Indian contemporary experiences which revolved around IIT's and IIM's.

Indian Popular fiction transformed into a consumer based industry. The writer writes based on what the reader (consumer) wants. The 'chick-lit' genre was becoming famous too as it catered the young females. Advaita Kala's *Almost Single* (2007) is all about female gaze. With catchy humour and bold take on patriarchy its sales figures baffled the literary pundits. Anuja Chauhan's *The Zoya Factor* (2008) was a perfect combination of India's obsession with cricket and romance. The 21st century also saw the resurrection of mythology in popular fiction. Writers like Amish Tripati, Devdutt Pattanaik and several others wrote about mythology in their works. Amish was a trend setter and brought self publishing to new heights. His stories were retelling of Shiva's legend and this resonated well with the reading public. His *Shiva Trilogy* novels were best sellers which carried a central idea of God in a human form.

In his popular article *Mass Civilization and Minority culture* (1930) F.R. Leavis says that it is the minority which sets the benchmark for mainstream cultural practices. This educated elite group of people dictates the taste of how things are to be made. This applies to cultural practices like fashion as well as literature. The second point he raises is the cultural hegemony of America which is taking control over other nations individual cultures. This also applies aptly to the Indian scene, where it is generally a well known fact that a person who speaks English is considered a gentleman and a highly educated person. In literature too we can see the same application of styles and techniques which were used in western fiction to the Indian side. J.D. Salinger's most famous work *The Catcher in the Rye* (1951), a campus novel has inspired many Indian writers. The novels of Chetan Bhagat apply those similar themes and as Leavis has stated we can see the cultural hegemony of America being Indianised. Lastly Leavis compares the competence of an average reader of the past to the average reader of the present and draws a conclusion that the former was more competent in reading than the latter. The reason he attributes is to the development of mass media and television.

Conclusion

Popular fiction in India thus became a commercial enterprise, i.e. Indian commercial fiction. It is no longer a derogatory term but is instead governed by market forces. Popular fiction is often looked down or frowned by academia. They differentiate between Literature and Popular fiction and often deem popular fiction to be not worthy of attention because of its simplistic prose. But the exponential growth of readership of popular fiction tells us otherwise and compels us to take Popular fiction seriously. Indians are buying books in hordes and the total market size is expected to be around Rs. 739 billion by 2020 (Neilson, 2015). It has come a long way since its inception. With globalization the barriers of language, culture and customs are being broken and Indian popular fiction is imbibing the western cultural archetypes and is continuing to grow and evolve.

References

1. Naik, M.K.(1997). A History of Indian English Literature. Sahitya Academy.
2. Aurobindo, Sri (2002). The Renaissance in India and other essays on Indian Culture. Sri Aurobindo Ashram Publication Department.

3. Khair, T.(2008). Indian Pulp Fiction in English: A Preliminary Overview from Dutt to Dé. The Journal of Commonwealth Literature, *43 (3)*, 59 – 74. https://doi.org/10.1177/0021989408095238

4. Nielson Book Report 2015 based on a study conducted by Nielson for Association of Publishers in India & Federation of Indian Publishers.

5. Chawla, Geetanjali and Mittal, Sangeeta (2022). Indian Popular Fiction: Redefining the Canon. Routledge.

6. Macaulay, Babington (1835). Minute on Education.

7. Leavis, F.R. (1930). Mass Civilization and Minority Culture.

CHAPTER NINE

Poetry of the Fallen: A Critical Approach on the Poetry of Jim Morrison beyond Global Pop Culture

[1] Dwaipayan Roy** & [2] Shuchi ***

1. **Research Scholar, Department of Humanities and Social Sciences, National Institute of Technology Mizoram, Chaltlang, Aizawl, Mizoram, India. Corresponding Author Email- brucewayne130@gmail.com.

2. *** Assistant Professor, Department of Humanities and Social Sciences, National Institute of Technology Mizoram, Chaltlang, Aizawl, Mizoram, India

Abstract

In the 1960s, the American poetic tradition was hit hard by the emergence of a bold, young poet named Jim Morrison. He later formed one of the most influential music groups of all time, named "Doors". His creative lyrics, along with rock rhythm, led to the creation of a series of classic poems. Morrison wanted himself to be remembered as a poet. But critics deny that. Most of the writings about Morrison centre on his bohemian life-style as a rock god. Even to this very day, merchandise for Jim Morrison continues to rule the charts in terms of sales, making him an icon in global popular culture. But Morrison never wanted to be worshipped as a "God" in popular culture, nor did he want to commercialize his art, lyrics, and poems. A little effort has been made to critically analyse the poetry written by Jim Morrison. That's where our research comes in.The objective of the paper is to showcase the creativity and genius of his poetry, often surrounded by the mist of blasphemy, criticism, and the culture of narcotics. We have employed descriptive research tools like critical observation, surveys and analytical investigation regarding the literary exploits of Morrison. This paper tries to cement Morrison's legacy as a poetic genius in the American literary scene breaking his image as represented in popular culture & the media of 1960s America. In short, we tried to rid the poet of deconstructive criticism and highlight his establishment of a unique poetic genre.

Keywords- *Jim Morrison, Popular Culture Creative Poetry, Dark Metaphors, Positivity, Innovation.*

Introduction

Jim Morrison was often touted as "the prince of Rock Music" by American media of the 1960s. His brief life spanned from 1943-1971 and he was mainly famous as the lead vocalist of rock band "Doors".At just 27 years old, he passed away in Paris, leaving behind an outstanding reputation as a rock poet. Rolling stone recently listed Morrison as the 47th most impactful poet & singer-songwriter of all time.The 1960s American literary scene was rocked by Jim Morrison's unique lyrical style.He refused to adhere to the typical social stereotypes and sexual taboos that the 1960s' traditional American culture imposed on his generation.Morrison's introduction of the psychedelic, sensual elements of rock poetry during the "Doors" concert was a spectacle that was never encountered by audience previously.In his poems, the social discontent and turbulence of 1960s America were amply depicted. While composing his poems Morrison indulged inhallucinatory images and metaphorical allusions and subsequently, they reflectedchaotic, depressing, and violent undertones.Morrison sought to appeal to poetry's fundamental functionality by upsetting traditional perception through the use of distinctive or alluring terms while also seeking for the unity and connection of all experiences.He is survived by his iconic psychedelic rock poetry and memorable theatrical acts on stage that still influence people even today.His poems were influenced by the sudden changes and transition in American and world history.If readers ignore the poet's socio-political ideas, they would find a scholarly analysis of world literature in his verses.His anthologies such as "The Lords and New Creatures," "Wilderness," and "The American Night" convey events, viewpoints, and ideas that are drawn from real-life encounters from the poet's personal life.Morrison's poetry explores subconscious feelings, sensations, and its subject matter is sometimes ambiguous.This feature of his poetry is frequently linked to the postmodernism movement.His poetic genius lies not only in the surreal ambience he conjures up for his audience, but also in the way he juxtaposes or twists words to produce unusual psychedelic effects. Readers experience a vision of apocalypse while reading the poet's verses. Morrison as a poet transformed poetry beyond a form of art and he employed it as a tool to defy conventional doctrines of conservative society and reality. Words, syntactical style and positive messages that he used in his verses affected and revitalized people's lives.He believed that poetry must transcend to become the force behind the development of social customs, historical records, and other forms of expression. Morrison was profoundly influenced by the literary tradition and ideas of Rothenberg, William Blake, and Arthur Rimbaud.

Morrison in Popular Culture:

Morrison in his lifetime never wrote poems or lyrics to become popular or wanted his creativity to be commercialized. Yet even today, Jim Morrison has become an icon in popular culture due to his rebellious persona and also in terms of topping the charts in the sale of merchandise,posters,t-shirts. To be very frank, Morrison always wanted his audience to get enlightened via his poems and philosophy behind his lyrics instead of being the "poster-boy" of his fans. American media often linked Morrison's bohemian lifestyle with his creations and undermined his poetic genius. That's where our research comes in. We have tried to provide a representation of Morrison beyond global popular culture and the negative image imposed on him by 1960s American media.

Method

As we are dealing with a deceased poet, we have solved the research problem using the descriptive technique. An analysis based on interpretation, survey, and critical observation of the Morrison's poetic works assisted us in achieving the intended goal. Researchers tried to dissect the poetic persona of Jim Morrison from his glamorous avatar as an iconic rock-star. The study would aid the reader in comprehending the poet's poetic vision as well as the intensity and depth of his poetry. This article addresses several queries like A. Are Morrison's poems really inventive? B. Does the verses of Morrison preach negativity? C. Is there seriousness and positive elements in the poetry of Morrison? D. Is Jim Morrison's poetry and creativity influenced by drugs?

Critical Investigation on the Mystic elements and Creativity of Morrison's Poetry

The Lords: Notes on a Vision (1969) combines poems, prose narrative, and philosophical thoughts. Morrison as a poet skilfully mixed Contrasting topics like film, death, and mythology in this collection. Critics may doubt the verse's authenticity, yet the ideas are profoundly intellectual. We must remember that Jim Morrison's poetry is rich in metaphors, aesthetic sensibility, and ideologies. In "The Lords: Notes on a Vision) the writing style is jumbled with its use of dark allegorical imagery and other personal components. The personal and historical references in the poems illustrate the transformation of reality into mythical fiction. The mysterious landscape created by the poet's imagination displays the psyche's inner world and its perception of the outer environment:

"Players- the child, the actor, and the gambler

The idea of the chance is absent

From the world of the child and primitive.

Chance is a survival of religion in the modern city,

As in theatre, more often cinema,

The religion of possession."(Morrison, 2021,81)

In the aforementioned lines, the poet rebels against the societal system that controls people's living standards. Instead of providing opportunity for individuals to enjoy their independence, the social establishment imposes strict dogmas and stringent rules on them. As a result, humans are obliged to live inside a predetermined framework imposed by an unnatural system. People are unable to articulate themselves freely in this circumstance, which serves as a roadblock in realizing their full potential as human beings. As a result, each individual's thoughts, emotions and sentiments are regulated and revolve inside the framework established by social institution.

"Door of passage to the other side, the soul frees itself in stride."

The poets' Blakean inspiration is reflected in the above phrase. While developing his vision of the human form, he was heavily influenced by Blake. " The Lord" is basically a metaphor for those in positions of power who bind us to our circumstances or to a fabricated version of reality that they have created. While revolting against all of this, the poet proposes a path for us to break free by going beyond what the poet refers to as "The Doors." This allows us to alter or transcend our realities or identities into a boundless, endless state. Critics like Riordan and Sugarman, Prochnicky believe that Morrison was constantly under use of drugs while composing the verses of "The Lords". However, if we examine his logic closely, we'll find poetic allusions to the romantic British writer William Blake. Our key argument for the former assertion is that they (the critics)overlook a crucial aspect of Morrison's poetry. Morrison never emphasized the usage of drugs to achieve the limitless or"Open kind of Existence" outlined in the preceding poem, "The Lords". Through the wings of poetical imagination, he preached the emancipation or liberation of the soul from the grips of authority systems, expanding his vision, identity, and reality into endless dimensions. The poet realized that people in this ordinary world are constrained by time and place, but that the power of imagination may overcome these limitations. It is not necessarily to dismantle every binary structure in order to reach the infinite. The poet says that this infinite dimension can be reached by looking at reality through the lens of the imagination instead of the lens of reason.Morrison praised the divinity of the human soul and holiness of imagination, which can help us understand his poem "The Original Temptation," stated below:

"To participate in the creation

To screw things up

To bring things into being". (Morrison, 1969, 7-9)

In the previous section we explored the process ofdeconstructing social systems that force reality on us leads to an infinite expansion of both our identity and reality. As a result, the poet focuses on the consequences of such an act in the poem above. Readers will notice a remarkable similarity of the above poem to "The West Wind" by Percy Bysshe Shelley. As Shelley prophecies, the west wind will bring death and decay in order to give birth to new life form. Morrison similarly suggests the destruction of the old order of things/age old establishments with terms like "To screw things up," while "To bring things back into being" denotes the revival of a new poetic or political order that would lead to renaissance. Through his verses Morrisons ushers the dawn of a new era of society devoid of social evil, corruption and path breaking poetic style that has the power to bring an art revolution in contemporary American literature.

William Blake believed that the only way to escape the pangs and pains of this world is through mental strength, commonly known as "The Doors of Perception." Through his poetry, Morrison endeavoured to raise the subject of life's purpose in the minds of his readers. His poetry was an attempt to give us a feeling of our existence or what it means to live in the truest sense of the term. Here, the senses may be seen as an imaginative leap beyond the realm of reason. His poetry attempts to elucidate the underlying subconscious needs /desire of humans on the highway of life, where reality and fantasy are entangled. The poet's spirit is comparable to those still yearning for the light at the end of the tunnel. The poet says that when we escape our dimension and pass through the "Doors of Perception", the world that greets us is a creation of our imagination. Morrison has always urged his readers to create their own realities and liberate their souls from the socio-political structure that preach rigid doctrines. Not only does he motivate readers to dismantle the old order, but also to build their own system for the "Self" based on individual requirements. The same idea is echoed in the lines of the poem "Break on through," which is essential to comprehending Morrison's artistic & poetic ambitions:

"You know the day destroys the night

Night divides the day

Tried to run Tried to hide

Break on through to the other side" (Morrison, 2021,1-7)

The above verses portray Morrison's passionate plea to transcend through "The Doors" to the other side. Contemporary American poetry of the 1960s experienced radically contradictory themes, such as "You know the day destroys the night/Night divides the day." His poetry portrayed love as a diversion that enslaves the present age. An attempt to distinguish between true and apparent reality is made in this poem. The other side" differs for each individual. The poet here celebrates distinctions between individual traits and recognizes the uniqueness that defines each and every one of us. As stated, before the motivation for breaking into the other side is varies from individual to individual. Spiritualism, music, art and a passion for literature might be the key to the other side, but ultimately, it's about discovering the ultimate truth of life. In the poet's case, rock & roll, poetry, artistic vision, passion for performing arts, imagination, and creativity all assisted him in breaking through the barrier to the other side. That is how the poet widened his perceptual boundaries and unlocked the other side. The poet exhorts his audience to go beyond the known and embrace the unknown, rejecting the falsehoods, illusions, and deceptions that come with today's fast-paced, technologically advanced world.

In his poems, Morrison attempted to include a variety of Christian, Biblical, and afterlife concepts. Incorporating all of these themes, he attempted to address moral challenges of everyday life. Stoned Immaculate is one instance:

"Soft driven, slow and mad /

Like some new language

Reaching your head with the cold, sudden fury of a divine messenger
Let me tell you about heartache and the loss of God
Wandering, wandering in hopeless night." (Morrison, 2021)

The poem opens with "I'll tell you this/No eternal reward will forgive us now/for wasting the dawn". This may be construed in several different ways. The poet emphasizes the need of looking back at the practical elements of daily struggles and facing life's adversities boldly. He emphasizes that, no matter how little and insignificant a problem may seem to be, it may serve as a source of motivation to confront life's larger obstacles when everything looks gloomy and hopeless. He believes that blaming destiny or others, or evading the pains of life, would accomplish nothing. To be successful we should must seek for possibilities every day, as each moment of life bring new opportunities. The poet's message is that people should not anxiously and interminably wait for everlasting bliss in the afterlife rather, they should strive to achieve so in their own lifetime by adopting a positive attitude against every adversities thrown by life. Morrison was not a religious guru, but his poems revealed his belief that good "Karma" would turn death into an "eternal recompense." The phrase "The Loss of God" alludes to a crisis of trust or losing faith. A faithless life is devoid of divinity. The poet here speaks of faith in one self. A person who lost in himself is comparable to a lost soul. A keen reader could see a parallel between this poem and Tennyson's crossing the bar. The poet, like Tennyson, believes in facing death boldly rather than being scared of it. The poet views "Death" as merely a transition into a new existence, as expressed by the phrase "Uncertain Dawn".

"Opening of the Trunk" is a poem by Morrison in which he compares his audience to a closed trunk.

"Let's re-create the world
The palace of conception is burning
Look. See it burn / Bask in the warm hot coals." (Morrison.2019,234)

He encourages readers to improve their intrapersonal abilities. Throughout the poem, the poet challenges his listeners to go deeper into their own identities or inner self. An individual cannot connect with anybody or anything when he/she doesn't know what they want in life or who they are as a person in the first place.When we liberate ourselves from 'Self-Ego,' we open ourselves to the cosmos, like an opened trunk. The soul is immortal and is not limited to the confinement of body, time, or place. The realization of the inner "self"/true identity will unite us with the oneness of the cosmos. This will help us break free of the chains of servitude and narrow confinement of the life-and-death cycle. The poet firmly believes that personal liberation could be only attained by rediscovering the true identity of the self. As the first line of the poem implies, this self-realization would help an individual to perceive world or reality with a divine tranquillity. Intriguingly, the poet's message resembles Vedantic philosophy, despite the fact that Morrison probably never studied Vedanta. Vedantic philosophy holds that self-discovery is the most difficult task. After this realisation, there is nothing more to explore.

Morrison, in his poem "If only I", strives to examine the pleasure and happiness emerging out of the tiny or smallest things of life. In the next lines, a sense of longing for one's early years is explored:

"If only I could feel,

The sound of the sparrows & feel child hood pulling me back again,

If only I could feel me pulling back again &

Feel embraced by reality again I would die, gladly die"(Morrison 2019,268)

Just as every individual yearns for his innocence, childhood and past, so does the poet. He wants to relive the celestial time of his childhood days and be inspired and delighted by the simple sights and sounds of nature, such as the chirping of sparrows. The majority of individuals consider childhood to be the finest time of their life. Indeed, the poet here addresses a universal issue that most readers would relate to. More importantly, he stresses the de-clattering of desire, thoughts, and passion. A child finds delight in simple things because they have the intrinsic ability to eliminate life's superfluous complications. The poet wishes to make this psychological shift from sinful experience of adulthood to purified innocence of childhood. As his fantasy fades, he returns to reality. He confesses that he would happily die if he could experience heavenly purity and delight of childhood once more.

Morrison highlights the simple act of trying to achieve something in his poem, "Power":

"I can make myself invisible or small

I can become gigantic and reach the farthest things

I can change the course of nature

I can place myself anywhere in space or time." (Morrison,1969,13)

Morrison strongly believed that human beings are blessed with inexhaustible willpower. He urged his audience to investigate and comprehend their own willpower and rise against unfavourable conditions of life. To the poet, the first step in accomplishing any milestone, regardless of its difficulty, is to strive or exert best effort that can be given by any individual.Through the first two lines the poet shows that any individual is capable of doing anything in life. As a result, the act of attempting is more significant than achieving the desired end point. The following poem's philosophy mirrors the thoughts of the great monk Swami Vivekananda. Swami Vivekananda said that one should keep striving until he or she achieves his or her goal.

"Riders on the Storm Into this house we're born

Into this world we are thrown /Girl you got to love your man

Take him by his hand

Make Him Understand

The World on you Depends" (Morrison, 2021, 527)

In the opening verse of the above poem titled "Riders on the Storm", the poet uses a distinctive approach to express life's uncertainties. He implies that we have no influence over our destiny while we are born. Our birth is predetermined by destiny or is beyond our control. The poet deliberately utilized personification to exemplify human life, as if attempting to calm a storm. The above stanza is a lament that expresses the sorrow and powerlessness of an individual's existential peril in several conditions in a complicated universe. Images such as "Dog without a bone" and "Actor out of Loan" reflect to people' fruitless struggle against nemesis or complications arising from modern-day consumerism (allusion to contemporary American society of 1960s).

To unleash the creative power of the unconscious mind, Morrison experimented with the illogical juxtaposition of gloomy or dark imageries, phrases, and metaphors. The following poem, "Awake," has an abundance of such surrealism:

"Shake dreams from your hair

My pretty child, my sweet one.

Choose the day and choose the sign of your day

The day's divinity

First thing you see."

In the opening stanza, the poem resembles a dream sequence in which the author urges his reader to relax and experience inner calmness. Readers are referred to as "My Pretty child" in the text. Essentially, the poet is addressing the whole human species here. There is some ambiguity in the meaning of the phrase "Choose the day" because of the poet's intention to embrace both good and unpleasant aspects of life. The poet rejoices in the fact that every day and every moment is a blessing in disguise since they provide us fresh chances to achieve. The metaphors used in the poem give us a 70s feel.

"And we laugh like soft, mad children
Smug in the woolly cotton brains of infancy"

The preceding lines certainly emphasize the adorable purity of infancy, yet neither it is mentioned whether the poet or the reader has attained childlike innocence. Pure is connected to cotton. Similarly, images of childhood and innocence are paired with the notion of purity.

"Couples naked race down by its quiet side
Enter again the sweet forest
Enter the hot dream" (Morrison.2021, 410-415)

The first phrase is a metaphor for individual liberty. Serious readers will take note of the opening sentence's startling contrast of imageries used, which depicts a quiet racing competition devoid of commotion. The last two concluding sentences contain explicit sexual innuendos.Morrison considered sex as something similar to a celestial union.To make it more lucid he celebrated the holiness of making love. He essentially desired that sex should be free from societal preconceptions and taboos.

5. Result:

Although Morrison indulged in a bohemian lifestyle, his contribution to poetry cannot be questioned. We have tried to lens the brilliance of his poetry in the below instances:

Stoned Immaculate-Christian philosophy's conventional conception of the afterlife is challenged by the poet. It is virtuous "Karma" rather than simple confession of misdeeds that converts death into an ultimate truth or reward. The poet exhorts his audience to confront life's uncertainties boldly so that they would be better prepared to face death when it comes. This philosophical thought or idea strikes deep into the psyche of readers. Accepting the unpredictability of life would result in accepting the uncertainties of the afterlife as well.

The Opening of the Trunk- Morrison presents us with this metamorphic critical work in which he reveals the soul's quest for redemption. The salvation of the soul is difficult. It is comparable to opening a locked box or trunk. In this poem, the author artfully links spirituality with literature.

The Hitchhiker- A killer fusionof spoken poetryand rock song. At first Morrison wrote Hitchhiker as a poem and later converted it into a song. When transformed into a song, it shattered all records. This poetry confronts the reader with his or her most primitive instincts.1960s America was stunned to hear poetry on stage during live shows.

Awake-This poem demonstrates Morrison's preference for ambiguity over standard rhyme. The reader feels as if he or she is visualizing a post-impressionist artwork. The poem's surrealistic impact is remarkable. The emphasis of the poem is on the free expression of desire.

Power- Readers who had lost hope in life would regain it after reading these poems. This poem praises the divine nature of determination and willpower. The poem's lines inspire readers to believe that everything can be accomplished in life by the simple act of trying again and again despite setbacks.

6. Discussion on the Poetic Influences of Morrison:

Morrison was a poet who always held the view that poetry preaches and delights by giving people opportunities to rediscover themselves. To neutralize the demons of his unstable soul, he engaged in perplexing and inventive literary endeavours. Criticism of Morrison's poetry is based on a lack of understanding of the underlying meaning of his work, which these critics ignore. As stated in the majority of the poems, including "Stoned Immaculate," "If Only I," and "Power," the poet emphasized on empowerment and explored elements of positive psychology whichhas no relation to marijuana or narcotics. Morrison has highlighted the infinity of human form (open and closed forms of existence) and the liberation of soul, intellect and psyche can be achieved only through poetic creativity or imagination. He encouraged his readers to exercise their creativity and discover their inner self, and not to be influenced by a hypocrite world that attempts to shape people's notions of their inner identity or self. Morrison's poetry intoxicates the imagination of readers to run wild and pursue the realization of their inner self. However, we must remember that Morrison feels that the only way to achieve the infinity of identity and reality is via imagination, by separating it from the static structure of society, and not through drug use. William Blake strongly inspired Morrison. Blake's ideology had a substantial impact on his poetry. Although the name of his band, "DOORS," comes from the "Doors of Perception", the term was adapted both from Blake's "Marriage of Heaven and Hell" and Aldous Huxley's "Hallucinogens". Morrison classified the human form into two distinct sections: 1 .A framework or system through which a person understands or realizes reality and self-identity, i.e., "closed form". 2. In contrast to the preceding stage, Morrison also discusses "open form," which liberates people from the shackles of a static or fixed life and so enables them to grasp the boundless potential of the human spirit. All of the aforementioned philosophies or ideas are echoes of Blake found in "No Natural Religion" written by Blake himself, who believes in the infinity of the self. Blake celebrated the free expression of desires of individuals in his verses. The "Identity" that Blake and Morrison speak of cannot be definedwithin a physical structure or framework. The individual's evolving perspective, desires, and mental/cognitive processes are closely related to the reconstruction of identity. In addition to focusing on the development of individual identity, Blake's philosophy also emphasizes its co-relation to the outside world. Human perceptions, in Blake's opinion, are similar to "Doors" that allow us to glimpse the "infinite," or the actual essence of the universe beyond our five senses.

"If the Doors of perception are clesened everything would appear to man as infinite. For man has closed himself up"- (Blake,1906,14)

Morrison and Blake both felt that people's perceptions of their surroundings were constrained by the conventional bounds or frameworks imposed by political authorities, educational institutions, literature, philosophy, and religious cults. Blake has always emphasized how crucial it is to open the "Doors" of vision /perception in order to see a reality that is genuinely "Infinite" and to challenge the rigid order that the authorities / social institutions enforce on us. To put it more simply, the key to a person's liberation from the static framework imposed by authorities and preventing them from fully experiencing the vastness and infinite potential of the universe, reality, and vision, rests in opening or transcending through the "Doors of Perception". The previous phrase implies that, persons portraying nineteenth-century England were effectively captives within the delusion of their own thoughts. As a result, they had established a close system of order unconsciously within them failing to experience the world's endless potential. The above thought is mirrored in Blake's poem "London," which emphasizes the reality that humans are controlled and influenced by fixed norms established by outside stimulation that are not inherent or innate.

Blake's term "Mind forged Manacles" symbolizes the trapping or indoctrination of humans, preventing them from thinking freely and spoon-feeding them the rules or method for perceiving reality set by an external entity. This is fatal in the sense that an individual's self-perception, reality, and the five senses are unable to connect with nature, fails to attain its true potential and unable to experience its infiniteness. Such lives revolve inside a rigid framework of static or superficial perception, reality, and dogma. The poems of Morrison that we discussed in the previous section bring out the positive psychology, Vedanta philosophy, and universal sentiment that heal and touch the lives of people even today. While drug use dulls the senses, Morrison's poetry is based on the idea that poetry frees people from the boundaries of their senses. The researchers attempted to dispel Morrison's reputation as a pessimistic poet by showcasing his literary brilliance and innovation. It is for the readers to judge how far the researchers have been successful in their initiative.

Conclusion

Morrison felt that only poetry and music had the ability to sustain global wars or any other catastrophe. Neither researchers nor critics analysed his poetry seriously. Morrison's intense experimentation with music, poetry, and philosophy, which ushered in a social revolution in the poetic and musical scene, will be reflected in every critical study conducted on the history of American literature, notably during the 1960s and 1970s. Morrison was a mystical poet with an eccentric style, like Blake and Rimbaud. He skilfully incorporated poetry into the rock music genre, indicating that he was ahead of his time. We must remember that the 1960s and 1970s literary scene in America was a mirror of the idealistic & romantic aspirations of the French Revolution.The successful incorporation of French romantic ideals into American poetry was accomplished by the progressive poets (1960s–70s) who ventured to create a new revival., and Jim Morrison was one of the major spark of that revolution.Thus, based on our research, we can conclude that there is no dispute about Jim Morrison's literary genius, despite the fact that he does not have his rightful position as a poet in American literature and till date remains just a global icon in popular culture.

References & Bibliography

1. Blake, William. 1977. The Complete Poems. Britain: Penguin Books Ltd

2. Blake, William.2017. The songs of Innocence and Experience. Britain: Penguin.

3. Cook, William. 2003. Jim Morrison: A "Serious" Poet? Accessed July 13 2021. www.Litkicks.Com.

4. Cook, William, 2020. Gaze Into The Abyss: The Poetry of Jim Morrison, New Zealand: Independently published.

5. Davis, Stephen. 2005 Jim Morrison: Life, Death, and Legend. USA: Gotham.

6. Densmore, John. 1991. Riders on the Storm: My Life with Jim Morrison and the Doors. USA: Delta.

7. Eliot, Thomas Stearns 1960. The Sacred Wood: Essays on Poetry and Criticism. USA: Ingram short title .

8. Fearon, Fayne. 2019. Six Morrison Poem that affirmed his literary genius. GQ Magazine Culture. Accessed July 13 2021

9. https://www.gq-magazine.co.uk/culture/article/best-jim-morrison-poetry.

10. Hopkins, Jerry, & Sugarman, Danny. 1980. No One Here Gets Out Alive. USA: Warner.

11. Morrison, Jim. (1969a). The Lords and the New Creatures. USA: Simon and Schuster

12. Morrison, Jim. (1988b). Wilderness the Lost Writings of Jim Morrison. USA: Vintage.

13. Morrison, Jim. (1991c). The American Night. USA: Villard publishing,

14. Nietzsche, Friedrich. 1998 Beyond Good and Evil. USA: Dover Publications.

15. Rimbaud, Arthur. 2005. Complete Works, Selected Letters – A Bilingual Edition. USA: University of Chicago Press.

16. Riordan, James, &Prochnicky, Jerry. 2006 Break on Through: The Life and Death of Jim Morrison. USA: HarperCollins Publishers Inc

Impact of Diverse Influencing Factors on Environmental Degradation and Managing Sustainability

Dr.Piya Das* and SajalKanti Das[a]

Corresponding Author's Affiliation:

*Dr. Piya Das, Assistant Professor, Department of Economics, Radhamadhab College, Silchar- 788006, Assam, India. Email: piyadas_2007@rediffmail.com

♦SajalKanti Das, Assistant Professor, Department of Mathematics & Computer Science, Mizoram University, Aizawl -796004, Mizoram, India. Email: mzut228@mzu.edu.in

Abstract:

Sustainable development is associated with negative externalities leading to environmental degradation. Environmental degradation should be controlled for long run sustainability. Increases in environmental degradation keep the economy away from sustainable development, while decrease in environmental degradation keep the economy closer to it. The increasing population and transformation of world economy from traditional to modern industrial economy has led to serious environmental concerns. The objective of the paper is to analyse the impact of various influencing factors of environmental degradation and to suggest remedial measures so that the sustainability in the environment is maintained.

Key Words: Environmental degradation, sustainable environment.

Introduction

Sustainable development means managing the resources available at present in such a way that it does not breaks the harmony of the environment and also utilizing natural recourses, living in ecosystem, dealing with the components of biosphere in such a way that in the future also ecology, biosphere, environment remains optimal favourable, hygienic, healthy for the survival life with more happiness and with sound health. The development will incur the consumption and depletion of natural resources and environmental components but the sustainable development ensure that approaching the development and economic growth in such a way that the consequence of today's action do not alter the ecosystem, environment of tomorrow and make it more worse for the existence of life. How the various factors of environment like the<u>water</u>, <u>land</u>,<u>forest</u> and <u>atmosphere</u> is dealt with, how well they are managed is of prime concern towards the essence of sustainable development.<u>Actions of human being are responsible for climatic changes and degradation of environment. Hence these human interventions and actions against the climate need to be estimated.</u>The regulation of sustainability involves assessing, estimating theoccasions and amount of human-induced reasons, actions for <u>changes</u> in the climate.Environmental degradation happens because of many factors like rapid population growth, deforestation, urbanization, etc.So for safeguarding the environment and maintaining ecological balance between humaninterventions in environment and natural environment, the role of every citizen of the country is very crucial.In every country governments must pay attention to reduce the environmental degradation. The government itself can find solutions to the problem of environmental degradation. The sustainability will be maintained if there isincrease forest area, utilisation of natural resources in a proper manner and to preservethe natural resources. To maintain a sustainable environment balance, many more issues are there which needs to be addressed properly.

Review of Literature

Several economists across the world have studied all the aspects related to environmental degradation.A few of the literatures are mentioned below:

Alam (2012) has studied the problem of degradation of environmental along with some socio-economic anddemographic factors for Pakistan. He suggested that when economic developmentis expected then it is crucial to reduce the environmental degradation. Economic development is a major concern and it plays crucialrole to achieve sustainable development in case of Pakistan.

Mohanty (2009) studied that land under forest have declined over time across major states of India. The study finds that there is a phenomenal increase in population size and urbanization. The population has increased tremendously with urbanization in relatively fast growing states like Rajasthan and Gujarat.

Costantini&Monni (2008) have studied the cause and effect relationships among economic growth, development and sustainability. They combined the Resource Curse Hypothesis (RCH) and Environmental Kuznets Curve (EKC) models by adopting economic development perspective. Their findingrecommends that the necessity of high institutional quality and investments incorporatedwith economic capital accumulation is required to make a sustainable development pathway.

Kumar and Rana (2000)attempted to study the causes of increasing Green House effect, Global temperature, tides in sea, etc. and discussed the effect of ozone layer depletion and ultraviolet radiation from sun. Forest area in total percentage of land area, annual water withdrawal, total and per-capitaincome and green house index are taken as variable to study the impact of economic activity on environment. The study reveals that the present day policies dealing with environment are inadequate and incapable of tackling escalating degradation of the economic environment.

Vaikunthe (2000) has analysed that there is close relationship between economic development and environment and both are vital for economic development. He concluded that the problems have emerged due to lack of environmental awareness among scientists, economists, administrators, politicians and decision makers. As a result of which all models in the past concentrated on the maximum use of resources. He further suggested that a proper balance between environment and economic development should be maintained by designing environmental friendly economic models.

Objectives of the study

Thestudyhas the following objectives:

1. To analyse the impact of various influencing factors onenvironmental degradation.

2. To suggest remedial measures for maintaining sustainability in the environment.

Methodology of the Study

The study is basically based on secondary data sources viz; Human Development Report (HDR) 2018, which is collected from United Nation Development Programme (UNDP) website. Some countries are omitted due to missing values. In HDR 2018, UNDP has ranked 189 countries, but only 111 countries are taken as sample for this study.

Then to analyse the impact of various influencing factors on environmental degradation, multiple regression analysis is used, where the environmental degradation (ED)is taken as dependent variable while percentage of forest area (FA), fresh water withdrawals(FFW),percentage of urban population(PURPL)are taken as independent variables. The following regression is the empirical model for the analysis as mentioned above:

$$ED1i=\alpha1+\beta11FAi+\beta12FWWi+\beta13PURPLi+u1i$$

Forest area (FA)is considered as one of the influential factor in absorbing the oxides of carbon and other greenhouse gases, which ultimately helps in reduction of environmental degradation. Forest Area (FA) includes temporarily un-stocked areas, due to human intervention or natural causes. But these areas are expected to regenerate according to UNDP. Hence higher percentage of FA will indicates lower amount environmental degradation. FWW can bedefined as a percentage of total renewable water resourcesto be withdrawn in a given year. Excessive withdrawal of ground water can affect the environmental balance and assumed to be positively related with environmental degradation. It has been found in the previous literature urbanisation and environmental degradation is positively related(Alam 2012 &2010). Here percentage of urban population out of total population of the nation (PURPL) is taken as independent variable. Urban population is defined as the percentage of population who are living in urban areas in a country.

Results and Findings

It is found that environmental degradation is negatively related with forest area and positively fresh water withdrawals. This is because the group of countries under the study are basically the highly developed countries and with the advent of development they have focussed on industrialisation. For this purpose coverage of forest areas have decreased and fresh water withdrawn has been increased in these countries. As a result environmental degradation increases in these groups of countries. Howeverthese countries have focussed on environment friendly technologies or green technologies and with the growth of these countries environment have not been degraded to a large extent. On the other hand with the increase in education people are becoming aware about the environmental degradation but they are not conscious about the way to minimise the same.

With the increase in income they are focussing more on industrialisation and as a result environmental degradation increases. As people are becoming educated but neglecting the issue of environment. They are not doing any activity which will directly or indirectly reduce degradation of environment (e.g. afforestation, less CO_2 emissions etc.). As a result environmental degradation increases. The increases in urban population thus lead to increases in environmental degradation.

To reduce the environment degradation and to motivate others to become more environmentally sustainable following measures are suggested.

- **Throwaway items should be replaced with reusable items**

- Carrying one's own cup or water bottle
- Instead of using plastic bags and plastic wrap, airtight and reusable food containers should be used
- Using rechargeable batteries

- Printing as little as possible and if needed

- For wrapping gifts, it is better to usecloth and tie with ribbon, as both are reusable
- Electricity when not in use should be switched off (e.g.lights, televisions, computers, printers, etc.)

- The waste bags should be recycled
- Awareness should be done on what can and cannot be recycled

Conclusion:

Eventually it can be concluded that the crucial factor of minimizing environmental degradation for all the countries as a whole are forest area, fresh water withdrawals and percentage of urban population. It can also be further concluded that if countries are employing environment friendly technologies, eco-friendly measures, green-initiatives and their environmental degradation is low then only environmental sustainability can be maintained and the biosphere, ecology will be left to the next generation with better optimality for life to grow and survive with happiness.The government ititaives and public cooperation is much crucial for environmental harmony and balance, so government and citizens should go hand-in-hand for the noble cause. The government of India has taken various safety measures for protecting the environment and attaining sustainability. Few of the measures are National Mission for Green India, Swachh Bharat Mission and Green Skill Development Programme. The various rivers restoration projects of government of India like 'NamamiGange Programme', with the objective of increasing biodiversity, balancing the river ecology, enhancing the quality of water.Similarly the other Government of India initiatives are Compensatory Afforestation Fund Act (CAMPA), National River Conservation Programme along with Conservation of Natural Resources & Eco-systems etc. Hence it can be concluded that government along with citizen of every country should take proper initiatives for reduction of environmental degradation. Both of them should adopt green technologies so that ecological balance is maintained and sustainability is managed in the environment.

References:

AlamShaista (2012): *"Does Environmental Degradation Affect Economic Development and Sustainable Economic Development? Case of Pakistan, Economic Development - Different* Perspectives"*, Dr. Maria Lucia Seidl-De-Moura (Ed.), ISBN: 978-953-51-0610-4, InTech, Available from:http://www.intechopen.com/books/economicdevelopment-different-6perspectives/does-environmental-degradation-affect-economic-development-and-sustainable-economic-development-case-of-pakistan

Alam, Md. J. B., Alam. M J. B., Rahman, M. H., Khan, S. K and. Munna, G. M(2006): *"Unplanned urbanization: Assessment through calculation of environmental degradation Index,"*Int. J. Environ. Sci. Tech. Spring 2006, Vol. 3, No. 2, pp. 119-130

Alam, Shaista (2010):*"Globalization, Poverty and Environmental Degradation: Sustainable Development in Pakistan"*, Journal of Sustainable Development Vol. 3, No. 3; September.

Colby, Michael E (1991): *"Environmental Management in Development: the Evolution of Paradigms"*, Ecological Economics, 3 (1991) 193-213 Elsevier Science Publishers B.V., Amsterdam.

Costantini, Valeria &Monni Salvatore (2008*): "Environment, Economic Development and Economic Growth"*, Ecological Economics, Vol: 64, Issue 4, pp. 867–880.

Kumar, Rajendra&Rana, R.K. (2000): *'Environment and Development: Some Global Issues'* in Environment and Economic Development by N. Rajlakshmi (ed.), Manak Publisher Ltd, Delhi

Mohanty. Soumya (2009): *"Population Growth, Changes in Land Use and Environmental Degradation in India,"*, Available from: http://iussp2009.princeton.edu/papers/91994

Vaikunthe, L.D (2000): *'Issues on Environment and Economic Development: Global and National Levels'*,in Environment and Economic Development by N. Rajlakshmi (ed.), Manak Publisher Ltd, Delhi

CHAPTER ELEVEN

Impact of Mass Media in Yoga Promotion

Moirangthem Mangalsana Sing[1], Dr Saugata Sarkar[2]

[1]Yoga Instructor, Sports Department, Mizoram University, Aizawl

[2]Asst. Director of Physical Education, Sports Department, Mizoram University, Aizawl

Corresponding Author Dr.Saugata Sarkar, sougata.babul@gmail.com

Abstract

The role of the media in promoting any activity has always been pivotal. The most effective and extensive form of communication in modern society is widely acknowledged to be the mass media. It follows that the media's impact on society's conception of physical activity and the social and personal values it promotes is undeniable. Mass media played a vital effect in the development of yoga. Yoga is the science and art of right living which come down to us since the beginning of time in India. The primary goal of yoga practise in the past was personal enlightenment; currently, the emphasis is on using it as a holistic therapeutic method for many somatic and psychological ailments. With the aid of the media, the entire globe is made aware of these advantages. The phrase "mass communication" refers to a method of distributing information to a sizable population. The growth and impact of the mass media, including printed publications and electronic media like radio, television, newspapers, magazines, and the internet, as well as social media like YouTube and Facebook, have been a major contributor to the global adoption of the yoga tradition. The field of media education offers a wide range of opportunities for teaching and research. Yoga journals, yoga-related news, articles, and programmes also has significant role in spreading the yoga message and its benefit to mankind across the world.

Keyword: Yoga, mass media, print media, broadcast media, outdoor media, digital media.

Introduction:

Mass media broadcast many productive information about our health, fitness, physical activity, selection of foods and many more information for many years. People are starting practicing many physical activities as they aware of their fitness and health. Yoga practicing has grown exponentially over the last few decades in the West. World Health Organization officially began promoting yoga in developing countries in 1978 with the recognition of its benefit to human race. Now yoga is widely recognized and practiced in whole world and also become a massive industry. This whole information is spread by mass media and people easily get them. Thus, we can know that there is some relationship between mass media and yoga.

Mass Media:

Mass media is a mode of public communication that simultaneously reaches a sizable population that is dispersed, heterogeneous, and anonymous. Additionally, it refers to media tools that are used to spread information to a large audience. Along with books, posters, recorded music, and other widely disseminated media, this includes the press, the cinema, radio, and television. The purpose of the media in our society is to inform, educate, and entertain people. People are using mass media more frequently as a result of technological advancements and increased awareness of it. People used it for self-education, entertainment, as well as for gathering news and information from around the globe. Many small or large companies advertise their products and share their messages through the media to connect with people.

The history of mass media was emerged with the performed of many dramas in a number of ancient cultures. The widespread manufacture of books was made possible by Johannes Gutenberg's invention of the printing press, which swept the country. In 1453, he published a Latin Bible as his first work. Some of the earliest forms of mass communication were made possible by the introduction of the printing press. It made it possible to publish books and newspapers on a far greater scale. The term "mass media" was coined with the invention of print media. Then, technology played a major role in the development of mass media during the 20th century till now.

Books, Internet, magazines, movies, newspapers, radio, recordings, television social media etc. are various form of mass media. Mass media can be distinguished into four major types, they are

i. Print media – it disseminates information through physical form. It is the oldest and easiest way of communication. It includes newspapers, books, magazines, pamphlets or printed journals.

ii. Broadcast media – it conveyed of information through electronically via media. It also called electronic media. It includes television, radio, films, or recorded music.

iii. Outdoor media – it is transmission of information as billboards, blimps, placard in commercial buildings, shops, subway cars or trains, sport stadiums or skywriting.

iv. Digital media – it is transmission of information through digital form. It is made up of both internet and mobile mass communication. It includes email, websites, social media site such as YouTube, Facebook, Instagram, twitter etc.[1]

Yoga:

Yoga is an art and a science of right living. It also technique for developing or balancing and harmonizing the body, mind and emotion. The word Yoga means 'unity' or 'oneness'. It is derived from the Sanskrit verbal root "YUJ" which means 'to bind' or 'to unite' or 'to join'. It means union of individual self or consciousness or soul or jivatmawith universal self or consciousness or soul or paramatma or God. Literally it means of balancing and harmonising the body, mind and emotion.Uniting the individual soul with universal soul is the expansion of the narrow constricted egoistic personality to an all pervasive, eternal and blissful state of reality. Many yoga traditional texts and scholars and yogis give different definition of yoga. Some of important definition are –

According to Patanjali Yoga Sutra, Yoga is defined as

"Yoga chittavrittinirodha". PYS-1.2

Which means Yoga is the cessation of the modification of mind.

According to Bhagavad Gita, Yoga is defined as

"Samatvam yoga uchchyate". BG-2.48

Which means Equanimity of mind is called Yoga

"YogahKarmasuKaushalam". BG-2.50

Which means Yoga is excellent at work.

According to Yoga Vasishtha, Yoga is defined as

"Mana prasamanopaya yoga itiyabhidhiyate".

Which means Yoga is called a skillful trick to calm down the mind.

According to Swami Vivekananda, "Yoga is restraining the mind-stuff from taking various forms"[2,3,4,5].

Yoga is an ancient tradition that originated from India. It is believed that yoga practiced have been started at the very dawn of civilization.According to the yogic lore, Lord Shiva is considered to be the first yogi or Adiyogi, also known as the founder of yoga and the first Guru or Adi Guru [2,5].The history and development yoga are divided broadly into five periods.

1. Pre-Vedic period - The study of the history of Indus valley civilization reveals that the practice of yoga was one of the significant features during this period. A number of seals and fossil remains of Indus Saraswati Valley (Harappan) Civilization with yogic motifs and figures performing yoga sadhana are found.

2. Vedic/Pre- Classical period–In this period teaching of yoga are found in Vedas, Upanishads, Epics, Teaching of Buddhism, Jainism.

3. Classical Yoga period – In this period the first systematic presentation of Yoga was introduced by Sage Patanjali. It deals with the path of Ashtanga yoga often we called Classical yoga. That's why it so called classical period. During this period, commentaries of Vyasa on Yoga Sutras and Bhagavad Gita ect. Are also came into existence.

4. Post-classical Yoga period - Hatha yoga was developed during this period. It is physical - spiritual connection and body-centred practices. Many great personalities of Nath Culture of yoga popularized the Hatha Yoga practices during this period.

5. Modern period – It is the period of many great yogacharyas and teachers spread the knowledge of yoga all over the globe. Swami Vivekananda's remarkable lectures in the West, especially in the Parliament of Religions held at Chicago in 1893, mark the proliferation of yogic culture in the modern times. He announced yoga is a scientific and rational discipline of attaining the highest potential in life [5].

Yoga isone of the six orthodox system of Indian Philosophy.Patanjali Yoga Sutra of Maharishi Patanjali is the authentic text of Yoga Philosophy. This basic text put forward the Ashtanga Yoga (eight limbs of yoga). It deals about the nature human being with respect to nature.It is also a broaddiscipline meant to unite thepsychological, physiological and spiritual to achieve a state of enlightenment or self-realization.Yoga philosophy is a valid discipline of Indian Metaphysics. It is the outcome of human understanding and insight gathered through thousands of years via practise in the fields of physiology, psychology, ethics, and spirituality for the benefit of humanity.The ultimate aim of Yoga is to set the individual free from the sufferings of life.It the different yogic texts, the ultimate aim of yoga is to attain/achieve self-realization / moksha / kaivalya. According to the yoga concept, one can reach that primordial condition by controlling their thoughts and clearing their minds [4,5].

There are many schools of yoga - Jnana Yoga, Bhakti Yoga, Karma Yoga, Raja Yoga, Hatha Yoga, Mantra Yoga, Laya Yoga, Kundalini Yoga and so on. All yoga schools of thought emphasized the importance of mind remains calm and balance of body, mind and spirit.Out of these schools, yoga has four major school namely Karma yoga (yoga for action), Bhakti yoga (yoga for devotion), Jnana Yoga (yoga for knowledge) and Raja Yoga (royal path of yoga). Raja yoga also known as Ashtanga yoga. The eight limbs of yoga are

- Yama – social discipline
- Niyama – self discipline
- Asana – body posture
- Pranayama – regulation of breath
- Pratyahara – withdrawal of sense
- Dharana – concentration
- Dhyana – effortless concentration (meditation)
- Samadhi – self-realization/ identification with pure consciousness[3,4,5].

Yoga is a way of life. Many medical scientist and researchers have already found the benefit of yoga to human race. They also proved the efficacy of yoga to human as well as to the society. Yoga is an important natural preventive measure to ensure good health. It maintains not only the health but also generates a sense of happiness and fulfilment by practicing physical postures, proper breathing, sufficient rest and relaxation, meditation, positive thinking and balance diet. In this modern world, using knowledge of yoga and taken it as an instrument, apply it to solve the basic problems of modern world [5].

Print Media and Yoga:

Print media is the oldest form of mass communication. With the invention of printing press by Johannes Gutenberg around 1440 in Germany, the revolution of print media begun [6]. Print media includes newspapers, books, magazines, pamphlets or printed journals.

- Newspaper – It is the one of the easy and effective way to transmit information to the people. It publishes written information regularly about current events in various field such as social problems, politics, business, arts and culture, science and technology,weather reports, sports and so on. Newspaper also plays a role for educating people and entertaining too. So, most of the people read the newspaper even in their work place or office. Newspaper agencies are doing business with the publication of newspaper. So, they track down the public interest topics and published it. In this modernworld, all the people have aware of their health and fitnessfor healthy living. World Health Organization officially began promoting yoga in developing countries in 1978 with the recognition of its benefit to human race [7]. Now, yoga is widely recognized and practiced in Western society also. So, the editors of the newspaper agencies start writing about health benefit provided by the practiced of yoga. They keep some reserved space or columnforhealth-related articles and fun facts of health tips also. In that space or column,they wrote not only about the benefit of yoga practicingbut also new scientific research finding in relation with yoga practices human body systemand how to practice yoga too. Additionally, they write about the autobiography of great yoga gurus, philosophy of yoga tradition, history of yoga also. This information makes public more awareness about the yoga and help in promotion yoga to entire globe. Many yoga institutes and yoga studios also publish their advertisement through newspaper. In that ways newspaper play an important role in sharing various information about yoga and promotion yogic tradition in this modern world.
- Books – It is also one of the important print media. It records the useful and important ideas or information and share it to the society. Book can give better impact to the society. It also plays an important role in social reform. In this world there is a lot books in various topics or subjects like science & technology, history, philosophy, autobiography, religious & culture, scriptures etc. Yoga is one of the Indian Philosophy, it has its own authentic book called Patanjali Yoga Sutra compiled by Sage

Patanjali. It deals with the principles of practice of all school of Yoga.The term yoga is found from the oldest Indian scripture Veda as Vedic Yoga [5].From that era, yogic tradition is transfer civilization by civilization into today's modern world. That means written information of yoga is come down to modern society passing through many civilizations and sharing its knowledge to different Indian scriptures and literatures of each civilization. There are many yoga relating ancient Indian scriptures. Some of them are the Upanishads (main – 108 such as Yoga-kundalini Upanishad, Yoga-chudamani Upanishad, Yoga-tattva Upanishad, Yogarajopnishad, Ishavasyopanishad, Katha Upanishad, Brihadaranyaka Upanishad and so on.), the Epics (Ramayana and Mahabharata), the Puranas, the Bhagavad Gita and the Yoga Vasistha. These scriptures taught spiritual knowledge as well as various method of yoga for gaining spiritual knowledge. In addition, there is also more books on Hatha Yoga tradition. Hatha yoga is based on the purification body as well as mind of practitioner in the preparation for higher states of consciousness. Some authentic texts of Hatha yoga are the Hatha Yoga Pradipika by Yogi Swatmarama, the Goraksha Samhita by Yogi Gorakhnath, Gherand Samhita by the great sage Gherand and another major text known as Hatharatnavali which was written by SrinivasabhattaMahayogindra. The Hatha Yoga Pradipika is well known one among them. It is believed that all these books are written between the 6th to 15th centuries A.D. [8]. Now in our modern world, yoga is widely practiced in western society also. B.K.S Iyenger is well known yoga master in Western World andhe was also the author of many yoga books on yogic practice and philosophy. Some of his famous books are Light on Yoga, Light on Pranayama, Light on the Yoga Sutras of Patanjali, Light on Life and Yoga for Everyone. These books are widely used and also have great effect in promotion of yoga in Western Society. Today yoga has spread throughout the west, with millions of people read books about yoga, attend classes or seminars, and do the physical exercises for which yoga is famous. For centuries these books have served as a resource for many aspiring yoga practitioners and spiritual aspirants too [9].

- Magazine and Journal: It is also one of the printed media which publish in a regular interval of time, may be weekly or monthly, containing a variety of subject matters such as health-related articles, financial & business matters, advertisements, movies& celebrities, religion, history, fashions, science & technology, and so on. In last few decades, many yoga magazines are publishing by different agencies and treated yoga as commercial purpose also. Some popular yoga magazines are Yoga Journal Magazine, Integral Yoga Magazine, Yogi Time, Yoga Lifestyle Magazine, L.A. Yoga Magazine etc. Yoga magazine break down yogaasanasto make it easier to understand or deal with, offer advice on how to practise more effectively, describe various yoga styles, connect yoga to social issues, and incorporate philosophy and nutritional guidance. Some are more interesting science-based fun facts of theadvantages of yoga in relation with modern life like how yoga treats stress and anxiety. These magazines have great influence to the common peoples as well as yoga aspirant people and commercial purpose like yoga studios.Different magazine agencies posted various pictures of many celebrities and models of practicing yoga in their magazine cover to attract the public. It strikes the mind of many youngsters, especially ladies because of the modeller's physical appearance, glow skin, and body fitness. Journal is academic and scholarly periodicals or serials publication but magazine is non-academic and scholarly. Printed Journal are any journal that is available in printed form. There is a lot of printed journals as well as online journal. It has different subjects, focus on science, medicine, legal interpretation and so on according to the respective subject. Journal publishes different articles of research study of various subjects. There is a lot of yoga related articles that published in different journals. They publish articlesabout the effect of yoga practices on the physical, physiological and psychological system of human beings. They also publish the capable of yoga, secrete mysteries of yoga, principles and technique of yoga in solving various problem that happen in modern life and various things from the scientific research study on yoga. These articles help the new yoga researchers and many yoga aspirants to study more deeply in the subject and also help in sharing the information yoga to entire world. Thus, magazines and journal also provide importance of yoga in this modern world [10, 11].

The print media publicize the various policies, programs and schemes of government to promote yoga; various news regarding with yogasana sports and various achievement to shed light on new emerging players. They also publicize any information or event in relation with yoga like International Day of Yoga, to open the eyes of the publics about the knowledge of yoga.

Broadcast Media (Electronic Media):

Electronics media is fast growing media in modern world. Unlike print media, they can broadcast any information or news much faster through the use of various electronic devices.They are important medium for broadcasting information or news today's world both urban and rural. They can influence many subjects like e-commerce business, science & technology, culture & religious, politics, social issues, environmental change, sports, health and education.

- Radio: It was invented by Gugleilmo Marconi in 1895. Radio transmits only the audio web, so we can hear only audio information. Older people have more habit in listening radio program as compared with youngsters. Many people have daily routine for radio listening, some people used to listen specific program or at specific times and some of them accompanying radio throughout the day. Many people like to listen radio for news, information, social issues, short drama and music. Radio also an important role in public education as well as it can have positive effect on well-being of old age people. In addition, listening of radio can get not only the information but also motivate one's mind, enjoyment of life, experience, relaxation, mood regulation and so on. Adding of yoga related program like health benefits, yoga related social issues, analysis of yogic tradition or books and interviewing various prominent yogic personalities may have effect the mass listeners. Discussion program with medical scientists, yogis and masters about scientific research finding on yogic practice can get much knowledge about yoga to listeners [12].
- Television: Unlike radio, which only provides sound, television programming also has images. This television's audio-visual nature leaves vivid memories in our thoughts, which in turn causes emotional connection. Television visuals are also more memorable because of the audio-visual quality. It now plays an essential role in our daily lives and offers education, entertainment, and information directly inside our homes. Additionally, there is a large number of the population is illiterate. Even though these people can't read newspapers, they can watch television. The information broadcast on television is available to anybody with a television receiver. It is the perfect medium for reaching a broad audience because of this. In today's world, a new generation of kids has grown up watching television. TV shows have a significant impact on how children act and develop habits. The majority of senior

folks also watch various television programs. They might be able to learn new things and change their minds as a result. These days, yoga-related television programming is available in various TV channel. It may provide more information about yoga tradition and science behind on it. It may also teach or direct us in the fundamentals of yogic practice.

Among the diverse mass media, radio and television take an outstanding position especially in terms of informal education because of their wide and vast range of audiences. Both are regarded as the top cultural and educational media[13, 14].

Outdoor Media:

Any media used for the transmission of information or the publication of advertisement that displayed outside the building or house is the outdoor media. It is used to communicate with people when they went out. Billboards, posters, blimps, placards are the best example of the outdoor media. Outdoor media are mostly used for commercial purpose for advertising products and making brand. They can attract public mind and make repetitive impression on their advertising things. Advertising of yoga related programs like yoga studios, institutions, yoga therapy centers may have more awareness to the public about yoga and its benefit to health as well as in society and also may help in development yoga in this modern society.

Digital Media:

The term "digital media" refers medium of digitized information that are transmitted by speaker and/or screen with the help of the internet.

- Website: With the advent of the internet, the scope of mass media has expanded, and individuals may now easily access it. Internet broadcast covered the entire world, not just a certain region or location. With the use of an input device, information is transmitted, and one can read, listen, or watch the information through an outlet known as a website. There are numerous websites dedicated to disseminating the most recent information about various aspects of daily living, including audio-visual quality. These days, we can simply find any information about yoga on many websites. Numerous websites also provide data, facts, and information in details about yoga. All the yoga institutions, studios, and centers used website to communicate with people. They put their latest information, notice, events etc. on their respective websites that people easily access through. In addition,there is also many websites regarding with yoga journals. They provide only the scientific research findings about health benefit of yoga and science behind it. It gives light to many yoga research aspirants as well as people to practice yoga for health benefits.

- Social Media: The fastest-growing technology in the modern period is the internet. The majority of people utilized the internet to interact, obtain information, and entertain themselves. It possesses all the traits of an effective, reliable, and competent media source. Nowadays, with the increase in smartphone users, individuals are more accustomed to using social media to keep themselves updated. Social media is internet-based social platform that exists online. They are interactive technologies that make it easier to create and share content across virtual communities and networks, including information, ideas, interests, and other kinds of expression. It is now a key tool for sharing material, drawing in new users, and increasing participation. Social media has influenced yoga in a variety of ways, including communication, educating, marketing, and so on. YouTube, Facebook, Instagram, Twitter are most popular social media platform.There are several Instagram accounts, Facebook groups & pages, and YouTube channels that provide information on yoga, teach different forms of yoga, and explain the fundamental principles of yogic practices. Yoga can also be learned by regular people by watching YouTube videos. Twitter updates with new study findings from yoga journals and information on yoga. Instagram and Facebook both shared many yoga-related videos and images. Numerous students and aspirants to yoga attend various live classes on YouTube, Facebook, and Instagram. Various yoga institutions, studios, retreat centers, and teachers/instructors have official social media accounts so they can easily connect with the public, post their official notification, and conduct online courses. Yoga is now readily practiced or learned at home without leaving the house. One of the best methods to maintain a healthy body, mind, and emotions is through yoga practice. People used social media to practice yoga at home during the Covid19 pandemic in order to stay in healthy and to relieve stress and anxiety [15, 16]. Different organizers upload and distribute various yoga event or programme promotional videos or photos to various social media platforms in an effort to strengthen public relations, cut costs associated with marketing, boost sales, etc. Social media has made it simple for us to gain, read, and watch information about yoga that interests us. The growth of yoga has thus been greatly influenced by social media too.

Discussion:

From the above study, mass media disseminated various important information about yoga. Print media, such as newspapers, books, and magazines, offer readers a wealth of information about yoga. Similar to how radio and television inspire wide audiences with the benefits of yoga. Billboards, wall printing, posters and placards all help in catching people's attention and generating interest in yoga. Additionally, the value of yoga in the modern era is also shared and taught through digital platforms like social media.Therefore, the role of the media is vast. Yoga is taken as a healthful exercise by the entire world, and the media actively promotes it. They increase public knowledge of yoga, demonstrate its benefits, educate people, displaying its positive value, inspire people, and encourage participation.

Conclusion:

From the present study, it can be concluded as there is a significant relationship with mass media and yoga. The effect of mass media in promotion of yoga is countless.

Reference:

1. https://en.wikipedia.org/wiki/Mass_media
2. Saraswati, SS. Asana Pranayama Mudra Bandha. Yoga Publications Trust, Ganga Darshan, Munger, Bihar, India, 2002.
3. Saraswati, SS. Four Chapters on Freedom. Yoga Publications Trust, Ganga Darshan, Munger, Bihar, India, 2013.
4. Iyenger B.K.S. Light on Yoga. Schocken Books Inc., New York, 1979.
5. Ministry of AYUSH GoI, Certification of Yoga Professionals Official Guidebook Level I (Instructor), Excel Book Private Limited, Delhi, 2016.
6. https://en.wikipedia.org/wiki/Printing_press
7. Mishra SK, Singh P, Bunch SJ, Zhang R. The therapeutic value of yoga in neurological disorders. Ann Indian Acad Neurol. 2012 Oct;15(4):247-54. doi: 10.4103/0972-2327.104328. PMID: 23349587; PMCID: PMC3548360.
8. Muktibodhananda S. Hatha Yoga Pradipika. Yoga Publications Trust, Ganga Darshan, Munger, Bihar, India, 2006.

9. Garfinkel M, Schumacher Jr HR. Yoga. Rheumatic Disease Clinics of North America. 2000 Feb 1;26(1):125-32.

10. Markula P. Reading yoga: Changing discourses of postural yoga on the Yoga Journal covers. Communication & Sport. 2014 Jun;2(2):143-71.

11. Webb JB, Vinoski ER, Warren-Findlow J, Padro MP, Burris EN, Suddreth EM. Is the "Yoga Bod" the new skinny?: A comparative content analysis of mainstream yoga lifestyle magazine covers. Body image. 2017 Mar 1;20: 87-98.

12. Krause AE. The role and impact of radio listening practices in older adults' everyday lives. Frontiers in Psychology. 2020 Dec 18;11:603446.

13. Guru BP, Nabi A, Raslana R. Role of television in child development. Research Journal of Humanities and Social Sciences. 2013;4(2):264-70.

14. Nazari MR, Hasbullah AH. Radio as an educational media: Impact on agricultural development. The journal of the South East Asia research centre for communication and humanities. 2010;2:13-20.

15. Sharma K, Anand A, Kumar R. The role of Yoga in working from home during the COVID-19 global lockdown. Work. 2020 Jan 1;66(4):731-7.

16. Wadhen, Vipin and Cartwright, Tina. 'Feasibility and Outcome of an Online Streamed Yoga Intervention on Stress and Wellbeing of People Working from Home During COVID-19'. 1 Jan. 2021: 331 – 349.

CHAPTER TWELVE

Social Media as Global Communication Platform: An Analysis of WHO Post Based on the Global Health Issue

*Riya Maurya,
Research Scholar, Department of Mass Communication, Mizoram
University, Aizawl, riyamauryalko@gmail.com
**Dr. Dheeraj Kumar
Assistant Professor, Department of Mass Communication, Mizoram
University, Aizawl dheeraj@mzu.edu.in

Abstract

Background: Since December 2019, the entire world is suffering from a crisis named Corona Virus Disease 2019 (COVID-19). It started in China and within a short period, it emerged as a pandemic and claimed millions of lives worldwide. The World Health Organisation World Wide to take immediate measures to prepare their populations and health systems through a coordinated international response (WHO, 2020a). Even after the two years of the pandemic, the WHO is continuously working to disseminate Health based information through its social media platform and websites to aware people residing globally.

Aim: This study aims to find the health communication strategy used by World Health Organisation to disseminate health-related information to a wider audience through social media. The researcher will find the user susceptibility towards COVID-19-related posts posted by WHO on its social media and examine its frequency and effectiveness in reaching the wider youth globally.

Method: This study is based on the Content Analysis of content available on the WHO Social media platforms including Facebook, Twitter, and Instagram within a defined time frame. The Codebook will be formed and data will be analyzed Qualitatively and Quantitatively.

Keywords: Health Communication, social media, WHO, Public Health, COVID-19, Pandemic

Introduction

For the past two years, COVID-19 is all around us. It originated in a small in city of China, Wuhan in December 2019 as a small virus SARS-CoV-2. It started as an epidemic disrupting the community and then slowly affected the lives of millions, devastating daily life and hampering the economic condition of a nation, it has become a worldwide crisis as a deadly contagious disease resulting in a pandemic (WHO Study, 2021). To combat this crisis WHO keeps alarming and updating the population regarding all the safety measures that should be taken If it is circulating in your neighbourhood, keep a safe distance, wear a mask, keep homes ventilated, avoid crowds, rinse your hands, and cough into a bent elbow or tissue. Also, ensure to examine local guidance in the area where you live and work (WHO, 2020b). This year in the month of May many countries reported an outbreak of Monkey Pox in non- endemic countries like Europe and North- America rather than in endemic countries in West or Central Africa (Nations et al., 2022). This became another global health issue, WHO is consistently working to combat this upcoming crisis by disseminating the precaution and safety measures about the Monkey Pox.

The global upheaval was much controlled by World Health Organisation by providing relevant information to the global audiences, they keep updating COVID-19 scenario and safety measures to be taken by regularly posting on their social media platform. In this crucial period many papers arose stress and anxiety among readers which result in abolition of reading and television watching culture at many places. This become difficult in disseminating vital information to the masses as media was major ignorant in that period.

In this work researcher provide the detailed analysis of social media post of WHO based on major global health issues. This study aims to find the health communication strategy used by World Health Organisation to disseminate health-related information to a wider audience through social media. The researcher will find the user susceptibility towards COVID-19-

related posts posted by WHO on its social media and examine its frequency and effectiveness in reaching the wider youth globally.

For the study the researcher has taken two study on broad COVID-19 and Monkey Pox. Consequently, in this paper researcher has perform the comparative study of social media Facebook, Instagram, and Twitter.

Review of Literature

During the initial phase of COVID-19, traditional and new media worked together to inform a large audience about the epidemic and global crisis. Even after two years of the coronavirus, several health organizations continue to update and warn netizens and citizens about the pandemic. Along the way, conventional media has delved deeply and reached out to a diverse range of audiences. The study shows people preferred source for news is New Media (26.3%), followed by Television (22.2%) and then radio (1%) whereas for COVID-19- related news people relied on (52%) of television news channels followed by (48%) people prefer New Media (Tarun Goma, Dr. A Ram Pandey, 2020).

The COVID-19 pandemic has demonstrated the negative side of media, including how misinformation spread through social media and other digital platforms is causing as substantial a risk to worldwide public health as the virus itself. According to a study on the dissemination of COVID-19 information on social media, 43.9% of both male and female respondents prefer to share "scientific" information. This finding appears to contravene the general trend on social media, where the most popular content is amusing, engaging, and emotional. More over half (59.1%) of Gen Z and Millennials polled are "extremely aware" of and can recognize "false news" about COVID-19 and approx. (35.1%) simply ignore the post.(Wunderman Thompson APAC, 2020).

Twitter, Facebook, Google+, YouTube, Instagram, LinkedIn, Storify, foursquare, Vine, Ello, and Periscope are the current social media outlets used by WHO headquarters. All six WHO divisions have a Twitter and Facebook presence, and many country offices are developing the capacity to do so as well.. WHO may drive traffic to the WHO website where more thorough and reputable content can be accessed by participating in social media conversations and spreading credible information through social media. The World Health Organization's main social media outlets, Twitter, and Facebook, now reach nearly 6 million subscribers daily with health information("WHO | Social Media,"2017).

COVID-19 has a negative impact on mental health in the United States. Researchers has explored how the virus impacts not just the physical health of people who are afflicted, but also the mental health of the entire population (Stainback et al., 2020). To fight the battle

with Pandemic, robust health Journalism is necessary. Thus, Health Journalism must be enhanced, particularly in countries such as India, where mainstream media usage is high but health education is poor.It should focus more on credibility, Quality, and relevance factor.

Fact-checking will be required of newspapers and television stations, particularly to debunk fake news, misinformation, and disinformation on health-related topics. A good writing and editing is needed on health stories with full-time, highly educated reporters and subeditors. This will help people and communities to recognise news story and will enhance information literacy by using the media to engage with them. This will assist people in combating the infodemic on their own, as well as reinforce people's faith in the media (Sharma et al., 2020).

Methodology

The researcher has used a descriptive research design to achieve the research objectives by using both the approaches quantitative and qualitative. The content analysis has been used to analyse the official page of social media this includes Facebook, Instagram and Twitter of time duration of 30 days. It is defined by (Krippendorff, 2004) as a research technique for creating reproducible and meaningful references from data to their context. This includes post only based on COVID-19 and Monkey Pox.

Research Objective

This study aims to find the health communication strategy used by World Health Organisation to disseminate health-related information to a wider audience through social media. The researcher will find the user susceptibility towards COVID-19-related posts posted by WHO on its social media and examine its frequency and effectiveness in reaching the wider youth globally.

Data Analysis

Facebook Analysis

	No. of Post	With detailed Post Length	Without detailed Post Length	With Emoji	Without Emoji	Total Likes	Total Comment	Total Share
COVID-19 & Monkey Pox	31	14	17	13	18	1,60,27,044	5,03,063	1,48,474
Others	38	21	16	22	16	65,989	13,088	22,145

Table 1.1: Segregation of COVID-19, Monkey Pox and others issues on WHO Facebook post

The table shows segregation of COVID-19 and Monkey Pox and other post from the official page of Facebook, WHO. The number of post related to others issues is more as comparison to COVID-19 and Monkey Pox. The audience engagement, Likes, Comment and share on the COVID-19 and Monkey Pox post is in millions and lakhs, much higher than others post, this clearly indicates that user is still concern and cautious about the upheaval of global health issues.

COVID-19 & Monkey Pox		No. of Post	With detailed Post Length	Without detailed Post Length	With Emoji	Without Emoji	Total Likes	Total Comment	Total Share
Image	Infographic	5	3	2	3	2	9800	4924	2983
	Graphic image	12	8	4	5	7	15991000	486142	223897
	Total	17	17		17				
	Total Likes	1,50,36,200	964600	1,43,52,500	16,48,300			
	Total Comment	425675	65391	394294	96772			
	Total Share	200885	25995	186075	40805			
Video	Plain folks	2	0	2	1	1	1744	815	597
	Expert View	3	1	2	2	1	6300	2481	2292
	Gif	1	1	0	1	0	2700	789	334
	Q & A	3	0	3	0	3	4500	3072	1832
	Media Brief	3	0	3	0	3	7700	4100	2796
	Documented	2	1	1	1	1	3300	1195	1288
	Total	14	14		14				
	Total Likes	6800	19444	8344	17900			
	Total Comment	1499	10498	2431	9566			
	Total Share	2433	7161	2508	7086			

Table 1.2: Detailed Segregation of COVID-19 and Monkey Pox WHO Facebook post

Enter Caption

The table shows detailed segregation of only COVID-19 and Monkey Pox WHO Facebook post. The post majorly of two categories Image and Video, where image was portrayed in the form Infographic and graphical form, whereas video-based post are in many forms, this include Plain folks, Expert view, Gif, Q&A based, Media brief and Documented (showing story) to connect with audience. The table also clarifies Image based post having higher audience engagement as compared to video-based post. The graphic based images gather more audience response in Image category, where as in video category Media brief collect higher feedback in all three forms Like, Comment and Share. Further, the post is been classified based on with detailed Post, without detailed post and With Emoji and Without Emoji. The Image post with detail catches higher attention but reverse in Video post without detail post get good response.It is been concluded that audience are more likely to prefer Image based post with much detailing to get adequate knowledge of the issue by their own reading as compared by engaging more time in viewing video-based post.

	No. of Post	Reactions							Total Comment	Total Share
		Likes	Heart	Ha-ha	Care	Wow	Angry	Sad		
Monkey Pox	10	18300	1309	3925	408	121	357	97	9104	6421
Precaution Covid-19	6	2211400	82201	114931	22789	8421	8396	82039	206492	95497
COVID-19 Update	3	4500	766	366	164	77	90	64	3072	1832
COVID-19 Vaccination	6	13776900	104423	169837	27938	27938	10125	33239	280000	127644
Misinformation	1	3400	123	506	28	9	23	6	783	1400
Discrimination	1	6700	214	948	135	25	49	29	2600	1900
Health workers	3	5200	664	84	117	10	14	6	704	1514
COVID-19 & Child	1	644	25	59	25	3	47	0	183	391

Table 1.3: Segregation of COVID-19 issues

The table shows major COVID-19 issues and a monkeypox covered by WHO on FB post. Monkey Pox is the recent issue which is covered mostly with 10 posts, the COVID-19 Precaution and Vaccination is second mostly covered issue with 6 posts. Along the WHO keeps on updating and reminding regarding the misinformation and Discrimination related to COVID-19. The post related to COVID-19 vaccination received higher number of feedbacks in terms of Likes, Heart, Ha-ha, Care, Wow, Angry, sad, Total comment, and Total Share.

Instagram Analysis

COVID-19 & MonkeyPox	No. ofPost	With detailed Post Length	Without detailed Post Length	With Emoji	Withou tEmoji	Total Likes	Total Comment
Real Photos	3	3	0	2	1	39,919	398
Graphic Image	2	2	0	1	1	28,848	578
Total	5	5		5			
	Total Likes	68,767	0	44,194	24,573		
	Total Comment	883	0	516	367		
Real photos	2	1	1	1	1	1,25,558	180
Media Brief	1	0	1	0	1	10,581	193
Expert view	2	2	0	0	2	1,81,717	973
Total	5	5		5			
	Total Likes	1,91,578	1,26,278	9,861	3,07,995		
	Total Comment	1026	320	53	1293		

Table 2.1: Segregation of COVID-19 & Monkey Pox Instagram post of WHO

The table shows detailed segregation of COVID-19 & Monkey Pox Instagram post of WHO. The post majorly of two categories Image and Video, where image was portrayed in the form Real Photos and graphical form, whereas video-based post is in many forms, this includes Real Photos, Media Brief, Expert View to connect with audience. The table also clarifies Video based post having higher audience engagement as compared to Image-based post. The videos meant by real Photos and expert view gather more audience response as compared to other category. In video category Real Photos collect higher feedback in both forms Like and Comment. Further, the post is been classified based on with detailed Post, without detailed post and With Emoji and Without Emoji. In image category all the post were in detailed thus having greater number of likes and comments and similarly post with Emoji are more thus having more responses as compared to without emoji. Moving to Video category more responses is gathered by detailed post and post with emoji as there is only one post with emoji. It is been concluded that Instagram audience with are more youth oriented prefer media brief authentic video post as compared to other forms.

Issues Covered	No. of Post	Comments	Likes
Monkey Pox	3	550	1,41,231
Long COVID-19	2	523	1,80,864
COVID-19 Precaution	2	412	32,368
Media Brief	1	587	10,473
Misinformation	1	104	11,826
World Humanitarian	1	53	9,861

Table 2.2: Segregation of COVID-19 Issue and a Monkey Pox

The table shows COVID-19 issues and a Monkey Pox covered by WHO on Instagram. Monkey Pox is the recent issue which is covered mostly with 3 posts, the Long COVID-19 and COVID-19 Precaution is second mostly covered issue with 2 posts. Along the WHO keeps on updating and reminding regarding the misinformation. The post related to Long COVID-19 received higher number of Likes and Media Brief received higher number Comments.

Twitter Analysis

COVID-19 & Monkey Pox		No. of Post	With No Hastags	With One Hastags	With more than one hastags	With Emoji	Without Emoji	Total Comment	Total Retweet	Total Likes
Text	Text	22	1	20	1	1	21	939	1841	3594
	Link	3	0	1	2	2	1	182	241	480
	Total	25		25			25			
	Comments		173	765	183	348	773			
	Retweet		81	1787	214	385	1697			
	Likes		168	3468	438	628	3446			
Image	Graphic Images	10	1	8	1	5	5	791	2526	4232
	Real Image	4	1	1	2	3	1	207	278	735
	Infographic	2	0	2	0	1	1	111	366	613
	Total	16		16			16			
	Comments		17	752	340	644	465			
	Retweet		89	2489	592	1759	1411			
	Likes		232	4188	1160	2993	2587			
Videos	Expert View	5	0	5	0	2	3	299	1159	1437
	Media Brief	2	0	0	2	0	2	134	380	758
	Q & A	2	0	0	2	0	2	160	259	442
	Plain Folks	2	0	1	1	0	2	113	205	396
	link	1	1	0	0	1	0	56	115	193
	Total	12		12			12			
	Comments		56	346	360	151	611			
	Retweet		115	1292	711	393	1725			
	Likes		193	1680	1353	719	2507			

Table 3.1: Segregation of only COVID-19 WHO Twitter post

The table shows detailed segregation of COVID-19 & Monkey Pox twitter post of WHO. The post is of three categories Text, Image, and Video, where text is in form only text and link. Image was portrayed in the form Graphic Images, Real Images, and Infographic, whereas video-based post is in many forms, this includes Expert View, Media Brief, Q & A to connect with audience. The table also clarifies Text based post are higher in number than Image and Video. It also shows in all image-based post having higher audience engagement as compared to video and text-based post. The Q & A based videos gather more audience response as compared to other. In Image category graphic images gathers more Like and Comment.Further, the post is been classified based on no hashtags, one hashtag and more than one hashtag post and also With Emoji and Without Emoji.It's been observed that there are only few post with without hashtags, many post are with at least one hashtags but in contrast many post are written without emoji comprising all the three categories.

Issues	No. of Post	Comment	Retweet	Like
Monkey pox	28	1567	2854	5277
COVID19 Awareness	12	789	2993	4558
COVID19 Vaccination	3	71	160	376
COVID19 behavioural	5	184	652	1300
COVID19 Precaution	2	22	69	181
Long COVID19	2	170	455	703
Misinformation	1	189	187	485

Table 3.2: Segregation of COVID-19 Issue and a Monkey Pox

In twitter more post is of Monkey Pox, as this is the recent epidemic which world is facing, along WHO keeps on disseminating awareness regarding the COVID-19 and for the COVID- 19 behavioural change as can be seen through the number of posts COVID-19 Awareness and COVID-19 behavioural.

Findings

In Facebook, the number of COVID-19 and Monkey Pox post are less than post based on other issues, but also it generates more feedback. The post which was based on a graphic image, detailed one and with emoji captures more attention as comparison to other without detailed length and emoji. The Instagram audience prefer video-based content as comparison to Facebook. In video category audience prefer post with media briefing, showing higher number of feedbacks. It's been also observed that more post is based on without emoji and are detailed one.

In twitter WHO has equally distributed their content in various forms such as text, image, and Video. The post based on text are higher in number, followed by Image and then Video- based. Overall graphic based image has higher number of post and thus higher number of likes and Retweet followed by expert view in video category.

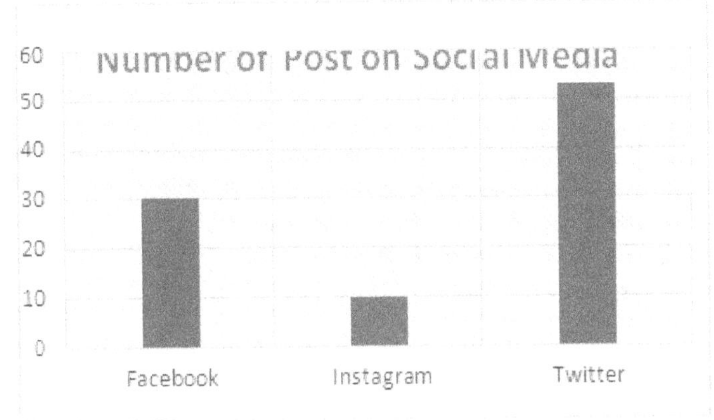

Table 4.1 Graphical Representation of Number of Post on social media

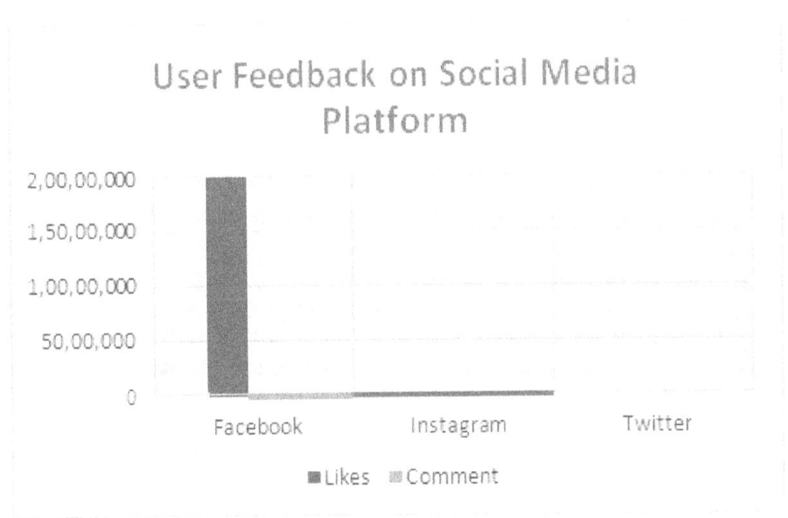

Table 4.2 Graphical Representation of Number of Post on social media

Table 4.2 Graphical Representation of Number of Post on social media
The graph clearly shows that Twitter has greater number of Post followed by Facebook and then lastly Instagram, where as table 4.2 shows that Facebook has highest number of likes as compared to Instagram and Twitter. Infact, Twitter holds the highest number post but have least

number engagement and feedback.

The present study revealed that Graphic based Image post is most effective in generating feedback. Besides, this study is totally based on WHO global health comprising COVID-19 and Monkey Pox provide exact content outcome of health-based organisations. This specialization will give idea the health based electronic firm to get an idea on descriptive data if posted contents and associated user's actions. Although several previous studies conducted on social media content analysis (Lai & To, 2015; O'Neil, 2016; Rahman et al., 2017; Ramasubramanian, 2005), none of them were based on specializing on health based issues. As a result, the study offers fresh value to social media content planning, particularly for worldwide health care.

Conclusion

From the above data of official Social Media page of WHO, it is evident that WHO tends to post about COVID-19 more frequently even after the two years of its outbreak. It is found that Facebook has highest number user engagement though having a smaller number of post as comparison to Twitter. Graphic based images is most effective in generating likes, comments and share on Facebook, in Instagram video based on real photos gather more feedback where as in Twitter media brief videos gather more attention in terms of likes, Comment and Retweet. Also, it is been observed that post with one hashtag and with no emoji are more and it captures more user attention. To engage audience on their social media WHO has nicely come up with various different forms of video-based post which includes GIF, videos with voice-over, music etc To engage global audience on the social media platform.

Reference

Krippendorff, K. (2004). Content Analysis: An Introduction to Its Methodology. In *Content Analysis: An Introduction to Its Methodology.* https://doi.org/10.4135/9781071878781

Lai, L. S. L., & To, W. M. (2015). Content analysis of social media: A grounded theory approach. *Journal of Electronic Commerce Research, 16*(2), 138–152.

Nations, U., Technology, P., Names, I. N., International, T., Names, N., Inn, T., Information,

W. H. O. D., Names, I. N., & Substances, P. (2022). *World Health Organization (WHO*

). https://www.who.int/

O'Neil. (2016). *Approved for All Audiences: A Longitudinal Content Analysis of the Portrayal of Women in Movie Trailers.* 159. https://scholarworks.wmich.edu/cgi/ viewcontent.cgi?article=1741&context=masters_the ses

Rahman, Z., Suberamanian, K., Zanuddin, H., & Nasir, M. H. N. B. M. (2017). Social media content analysis "study on brand posts of electronics companies." *Journal of Engineering and Applied Sciences*, *12*(1), 87–94. https://doi.org/10.3923/jeasci.2017.87.94

Ramasubramanian, S. (2005). A content analysis of the portrayal of India in films produced in the west. *Howard Journal of Communications*, *16*(4), 243–265. https://doi.org/10.1080/10646170500326533

Sharma, D. C., Pathak, A., Chaurasia, R. N., Joshi, D., Singh, R. K., & Mishra, V. N. (2020). Fighting infodemic: Need for robust health journalism in India. *Diabetes & Metabolic Syndrome*, *14*(5), 1445. https://doi.org/ 10.1016/J.DSX.2020.07.039

Stainback, K., Hearne, B. N., & Trieu, M. M. (2020). COVID-19 and the 24/7 News Cycle: Does COVID-19 News Exposure Affect Mental Health?: *Https://Doi.Org/10.1177/23780231209069339*, 6. https://doi.org/10.1177/23780231209069339

Tarun Goma, Dr. A Ram Pandey, D. B. S. (2020). *Representation and usage of media during Covid-19.*

WHO. (2017). WHO | Social media. *WHO.* http://www.who.int/dco/ strategy/functions/social- media/en/

WHO. (2020a). *COVID-19 Public Health Emergency of International Concern (PHEIC) Global research and innovation forum.* https://www.who.int/publications/m/item/covid-   19-public-health- emergency-of-international-concern-(pheic)-global-research-and- innovation-forum

WHO. (2020b). *When and How to Use Masks.* World Health Organization.   https://www.who.int/emergencies/diseases/novel- coronavirus-2019/advice-for- public/when-and-how-to-use-masks

WHO Study, J. W.-C. (2021). WHO-convened Global Study of Origins of SARS-CoV-2.

Joint WHO-China Study Team Report, February, 120.

Wunderman Thompson APAC. (2020). *Social Media & COVID-19: A Global Study of Digital Crisis Interaction among Gen Key Insights.* https://cdn.who.int/media/docs/default-source/epi-win/who-covid- youth- survey.pdf?sfvrsn=665ad659_5

Links https://www.facebook.com/WHO
https://www.instagram.com/who/?hl=en
https://twitter.c